The Detour Diaries

Women's Voices on Career Disruption

7	Career Detours
22	The Motherhood Detour
47	Detour through Devastation
66	The Karmic Detour
86	Gendered Roadblocks
112	The Unmapped Path

I dedicate this book to women everywhere who carry invisible weight while building extraordinary lives.

The women who shared their stories with me revealed both the burden and privilege of combining career with womanhood.

Their trust in sharing these precious stories was a gift I don't take lightly.

In our suffering and success, we find common ground and strength.

Julie Sack

Career Detours

Feminist/Realist: Finding a Place in the Conversation

There is an unwritten rule that writing a book about women's experiences should happen through a feminist lens. This made me question my own feminist standpoint before writing, and then continually question it throughout the process. I acknowledge that there is no single approach to writing a book like this which would be considered correct by all, given the many layers of women's experiences that intersect historically, socially and culturally.

I must be at least some type of feminist if I am outraged by issues of gender equality (which I am), but I am certainly not one of the placard-holding, bra-burning types. Feminism has too often been portrayed as extreme and unreasonable. Why can't it be subtle but steadfast? Sensible and measured? In my experience, the work of feminism happens through daily interactions, actions and reactions. It's building mindsets and values through critical questioning, creating boundaries, and challenging boundaries.

The world brims with inequities that demand challenge, yet change rarely arrives in thunderous moments of dramatic uprising. More often, change seeps through the quiet cracks of everyday resistance. Let's be honest: protesting is a luxury few can afford. While passionate activists occupy the frontlines, most women navigate complex professional landscapes through subtle workplace negotiations and small but powerful acts of everyday defiance.

Choosing between being a feminist or a realist isn't necessary. These perspectives are complementary strategies. Some days, we roar. Other days, we strategise. Most days, we simply persist. The woman quietly asserting her worth in a meeting room is no less a feminist than the one leading a protest. A mother restructuring her work schedule to balance care responsibilities is revolutionary in her own right.

Am I a feminist? A realist? I am both. I am neither. I am simply a woman determined to carve space, acknowledge change, and share the gift of women's stories that have been given to me.

My perspective carries the unmistakable imprint of privilege—I'm a cisgender, heterosexual, white, educated woman from a stable household in a politically secure country, with access to education, healthcare, and vast opportunity. These substantial advantages have shaped my ability to see, understand, and interpret. My feminism is as much a product of these privileges as it is of my lived experiences and hardships. I offer my perspective not as universal truth, but as one voice in an essential conversation, filtered through my particular view of the world—a foggy lens, imperfect and incomplete.

This navigation between feminist ideals and pragmatic realism reflects the larger historical journey of feminism itself. Multiple waves have advocated for a fairer world, chipping away at seemingly unbreakable societal structures. These victories represent visible progress, but the invisible burdens of gender bias continue to weigh down women's professional lives like a bag of invisible rocks.

Women choosing careers today carry these invisible rocks while navigating an obstacle course that differs fundamentally from men's paths. Women's career trajectories have never mirrored men's, particularly in how they respond to disruption and detour. This isn't just a feminist perspective—it's a realistic account of systemic patterns. Life events completely unravel women's careers with greater ferocity and longer-lasting consequences than their male counterparts. That women continue pursuing professional aspirations despite carrying invisible rocks speaks to their extraordinary resilience. The pragmatist in me sees this reality; the feminist in me refuses to accept it as inevitable or unconquerable.

These pages reflect *my* truth through *my* particular lens—imperfect, but honest. The experiences shared here will resonate differently with each reader. Some will see themselves reflected perfectly, others will catch just a glimpse of recognition. I invite you to use your own lens to navigate these stories, adding your understanding to this collective exploration of women's professional resilience.

The Burden of Invisible Rocks

Navigating a career as a woman is challenging. The modern world professes equality, yet it's an inconsistent and unpolished version of equality that is difficult to define. Let's think about the obstacle course. Imagine that your life and career are the course. There are ups and downs. There are shortcuts and detours. Many of the obstacles are known, but many are unexpected or more challenging than expected.

Women navigating careers are running that obstacle course while carrying a bag full of invisible rocks. These rocks aren't just something women choose to carry. They're a weight inherited from generations of unequal expectations—passed down through family stories, societal rules, and deeply ingrained cultural messages about what it means to be a woman. There's a series of hurdles, twists, and turns that demand resilience and determination, yet the woman must do this while she is weighed down carrying the rocks. The obstacle course includes many known challenges, like the rising cost of living and choosing the right career path. It also contains many unanticipated challenges. Women running the course encounter gender biases, pay gaps, and glass ceilings and so much more. Like when a women is expected to just nod and smile while she pretends none of this impacts her. No one sees the emotional energy expended, the delicate balance of maintaining professional composure while managing her womanly burdens.

The rocks women carry will sometimes be so heavy that an obstacle can't be conquered. Sometimes extra rocks get thrown in for no apparent reason. These rocks are not separate. They interlock, they merge, they amplify each other. A woman doesn't simply carry one rock, but a complex, interconnected load that shifts and changes with every professional breath.

Every now and then she can put a few down, or a few fall out and lighten the load, or someone helps carry the rocks for a time. But the rocks can never be all put down. The load MUST be carried. Carrying the invisible rocks of womanhood isn't optional. It's a sociocultural, inherited and biological burden which exposes multiple layers of privilege and social advantage, as well as layers of inequity and disadvantage. Privilege does allow for lighter rocks in more stylish bags, but it is still a load to carry. And here is the fun part—women need to carry the invisible load all while appearing that they are not weighed down at all. They need to carry it further, faster, higher, without complaint, all while maintaining the appearance of having no burden at all. Just because they are women.

If this sounds unappealing, pause and listen closely. This is not a chronicle of tragedy, or a cry for sympathy for all the downtrodden and burdened women. Not a single bra was burned in the writing of this book. It is a celebration of strength. Yes, the rocks are heavy, but they are also the raw material and the building blocks of something extraordinary. It's not all hardship and trudgery. Each moment of kindness and support is a collective lifting of rocks, a shared understanding that no woman should carry her burden alone.

There are times a woman feels so accomplished and proud for being able to carry her rocks the way she has. Sometimes the woman becomes so strong the rocks feel light. Carrying rocks your whole life is bound to make you stronger- isn't it? This book aims to capture, pragmatically, that strength. That while womanhood is riddled with barriers, it is also experienced with hope and resilience.

The Unequal Distribution of the Burden of Care

Perhaps it stems from women's inherent strength. Or perhaps it is the result of a complex social tapestry of gender inequity. An undeniable fact remains: women bear significantly more care responsibilities. Consider the numbers: around 70% of carers for people with a disability are women. More of the caregiving for small children is done by women. Historically, it has been women who care for their elderly parents. The parents often come from a generation with specific cultural expectations about burdening male children, who they perceive as leading more important lives. Their male children are seen as patriarchs, building and managing their own 'mini-empires'. The unspoken message is clear: care work is women's work. Behind the dry statistics lies a deeply personal narrative of sacrifice and resilience. These aren't just numbers—they represent millions of individual stories of daily commitment.

This unequal distribution of care in our society is known as the 'burden of care'. While various social reform initiatives—including paid parental leave and flexible work provisions—attempt to encourage more men to take up caring responsibilities, the lived reality remains unchanged. Women continue to juggle the majority of care work, but this juggling comes at a personal and professional cost.

The professional penalties are systematic and deeply entrenched. Women are penalised with fewer opportunities for promotion. They end up with less available time to pursue career advancements. They have reduced chances for upskilling and retraining. To manage their care responsibilities, women often make significant professional sacrifices. They accept roles that offer less job security, lower compensation, and poorer working conditions. Each compromise creates a silent tension between personal responsibility and professional aspiration.

These are not individual choices, but a reflection of a broader societal structure that continues to view care as predominantly women's responsibility. But is this all bad? Caregiving can be incredibly rewarding. Overcoming (or accepting) these obstacles (or seeing them as gifts), having the tenacity needed to break through (or trying to embrace) societal barriers requires grit and resilience, both individually and as a collective of women. Does feminism have to mean fighting every difference in societal expectations?

The burden of care is precisely where support systems become essential so that inequity does not remain a feminist argument. The generations of feminists who came before us created foundations upon which today's women stand—their sacrifices making visible what was once ignored, their voices amplifying what was once silenced. Thank you, feminists of the past. Historical victories, while significant, haven't eliminated the need for contemporary solidarity. Recognition of the reality of caregiving roles remains fundamental.

The specific challenges women face when their careers stumble or veer completely off expected paths must be seen clearly, not as isolated personal failures but as manifestations of broader patterns. When careers derail from original aspirations, be it due to caregiving responsibilities or other reasons, women are carried much further off course, with fewer pathways back to their intended destination. The options narrow, the obstacles multiply, the invisible rocks grow heavier.

Whether through personal choice, unexpected life circumstances, or those persistent undercurrents of inequity we collectively pretend don't exist, women's experience of career disruption differs fundamentally from men's. The same qualities—strength, endurance, resilience, patience—required by anyone navigating a successful professional journey take on different dimensions for women.

With their invisible bags of rocks, women must chart different routes, develop different strategies, and draw upon different resources. Not better or worse—simply, unavoidably—different.

The Sound of Change

Listen carefully on a quiet evening, and you might hear two distinct sounds. One belongs the raging feminists screaming out to the world their desires for career equality, their calls for career equality echoing with intensity. The other is a more subdued sound that you have to listen more carefully to hear—the frustration of realists who recognise how far we are from true equality. Both sounds are voices that share a crucial mission: dismantling the barriers of unconscious bias and uneven care distribution. Their ultimate goal is transformative: creating a world where professional potential is not constrained by gender. Yet, they diverge in their fundamental approach.

The first, louder perspective focuses on achieving despite gender. This view sees gender as an active barrier to be confronted and overcome. Advocates identify and challenge current systemic inequities while creating immediate pathways for women's advancement. They develop strategies to navigate existing discriminatory structures and empower women to succeed within the current system. This approach acknowledges the reality of today's gender-biased world and works to create success despite these obstacles by overcoming oppression.

The second, quieter perspective envisions achieving without gender. This approach looks toward a future where gender becomes irrelevant in professional contexts. Proponents work on reimagining societal structures and eliminating the very mechanisms that create gender-based disparities. They focus on creating environments where professional potential is determined by skill, not gender, and transforming fundamental social and professional paradigms. Rather than navigating existing bias, they seek to dismantle it completely.

Both perspectives are not opposing forces, but complementary strategies working towards the same ultimate goal of gender equity. The tension lies in the methodology: Should we fight within the existing system, or completely reimagine it? Life events that disrupt career paths point to a basic truth: gender significantly shapes both the experience of disruption and the journey back from it. In moments of navigation and restoration, theoretical debates fade. What remains is fundamental human desire for fairness, justice, and the opportunity to chart one's own course. Sometimes, that desire might just make you want to scream. If you have experienced even some of what the women interviewed for this book have experienced, you'll understand.

The big battles may seem settled—women can vote, wear pants, and occupy spaces once forbidden. But the war is far from over. Gender-based violence continues to cast its long and sinister shadow. Reproductive rights remain a moral and political battleground. Women's fundamental autonomy seems to be constantly under negotiation.

The gender debate isn't an abstract political debate. It is a lived reality that shape women's daily existence. While many visible barriers have been dismantled, the invisible ones persist with remarkable tenacity. Women navigate a complex landscape where the burden of care weighs heavily, the gender pay gap silently erodes economic potential, unconscious bias lurks in every professional corridor, and career aspirations whisper to escape from layers of systemic constraint. These invisible obstacles create a professional terrain that requires constant vigilance and adaptation, forcing women to expend energy navigating barriers that their male counterparts never encounter.

"Stand up!" you might say. But when exactly are women supposed to be full-time feminists? Between carrying invisible rocks, managing unequal responsibilities, and screaming silently about unrealised potential, there's little room left for organised resistance. The revolution happens in stolen moments, in the daily act of simply continuing to exist and strive in a world that isn't quite as ready for equity as it would like to think.

Stories that Matter

Life throws curveballs with remarkable and ruthless precision—be it illness, caregiving responsibilities, workplace injuries, or toxic work environments. These challenges test the very fabric of professional resilience, revealing strengths often hidden in daily routines. While such disruptions are not exclusive to women, this book illuminates the uniquely female navigation of professional upheaval. Through the stories of these remarkable women, we explore a landscape of career disruption that is at once intensely personal and universally resonant.

These are not just stories of setbacks, but narratives of extraordinary courage. Each account brings vivid insight into the full spectrum of anxieties, fears, emotions, and expectations surrounding life-altering professional experiences. Some stories conclude with triumph, others remain unfolding journeys, but each offers insight and wisdom.

The women interviewed shared their experiences with remarkable generosity—revealing how they confronted challenges, reimagined possibilities, and ultimately reclaimed their personal and professional identities. Their diverse experiences converge on a powerful truth: resilience is not about avoiding disruption, but about embracing it.

Not all stories have happy endings, and not all have reached their end. Each story illuminates something viatl: these women are not just survivors. They are the architects of their own remarkable comebacks. The career disruptions in this book defy simple categorisation. Some stories shock with their intensity, while others whisper of more low-key professional derailments. This is not a hierarchy of pain. It is not a competition of whose experience cuts deepest. Each disruption is unique. Be it a workplace injury, a prolonged illness, a caregiving responsibility—each represents a moment when a woman's professional path detours from its expected trajectory. The magnitude of the detour matters less than the human experience of navigation, of resilience, of finding one's way back.

In these interviews, vulnerability found a safe harbor. Women shared their most intimate professional challenges without fear of judgement, their identities carefully protected. They offered their stories not as performances of suffering, but as acts of generosity. This book bears witness to shared experience. It speaks to every woman whose career has slipped away, who has battled to reclaim her professional identity, who has wondered if her story counts. It whispers: your story does matter. Your disruption is real. Your journey is worthy.

The gift is not in the comparison, but in the connection. Readers will find pieces of themselves, and of those they know, scattered through these pages—fragments of fear, echoes of resilience, sparks of hope. Some will recognise their own invisible rocks. Others will see clearly, perhaps for the first time, the weight others carry. These are not just stories. They are bridges of understanding, compassion, and ultimately our strength.

The Motherhood Detour

The Transformative Shift into Motherhood

Motherhood is the invisible force that reshapes women's professional landscapes, often without warning or apology. It alters career trajectories in ways not many can predict, creating a seismic shift that recalibrates every aspect of a woman's professional and personal existence. The extraordinary feat of creating human life while completely restructuring one's identity becomes almost invisible, treated with a casual dismissiveness that belies its true transformative impact. This isn't just a momentary pause in a career—it's the most widespread career disruptor that women face, and its commonality doesn't make it less significant. If anything, its prevalence makes it more important to understand.

More than half of the women I interviewed for this book are mothers, reflecting an unavoidable reality: women's bodies are the ones that experience pregnancy, give birth, and undergo postpartum recovery. These physical realities cannot be delegated or shared. Even the most supportive partners and co-parents cannot experience the biological aspects of pregnancy, childbirth, postpartum recovery, or breastfeeding. They can provide invaluable support, but these experiences remain solely with the birthing parent. And in truth, most wouldn't choose to take on these physical aspects even if they could.

Having a perfectly healthy, normal pregnancy takes a woman out of her job for a few months at minimum. Even with an Instagram-worthy post-partum recovery, the experience remains exhausting and life-altering. For a woman's return to work to be seamless, the stars must align perfectly: a rock-solid support system, a unicorn baby who sleeps and feeds like clockwork, childcare that's both excellent and affordable, a psychologically safe workplace with flexible policies, and a manager who actually gets it. Let's throw in a cleaning service and assume her work wardrobe magically fits her post-pregnancy body. Only then might she glide back into her role with confidence, grace, and agility.

When all the stars align, it appears as though she never left—as though the invisible rocks she carries with one arm, infant balanced in the other, weigh nothing at all. She becomes that mythical creature: the supermum, the woman who can do it all without showing strain. The cruel irony for women trying to maintain a career while concurrently raising a family is that they're simultaneously bombarded with cultural messaging suggesting they should effortlessly excel at both motherhood and career. For all the work that's been done on equality, it is sometimes accused of going too far the opposite way, promoting an unachievable superwoman ideal. This was exacerbated by the 'yummy mummy' movement that dominated social media feeds for so long—attempting to show evidence that you really can have it all. All this did was reaffirm to most women that they were spectacularly failing at motherhood, life and career.

The pressure to excel in every aspect of life—effortlessly balancing career success, perfect parenting, and personal fulfillment—has left many women feeling exhausted and inadequate. This unattainable ideal has deepened the gap between expectation and reality, making it harder for women to acknowledge their struggles without feeling like failures. The truth is, no one can truly 'have it all' in the way social media portrays, and the pursuit of this illusion often leads to burnout rather than the happiness it promises.

Reality tells a different story. If even one of these odds are not in her favour—a baby who doesn't sleep through the night, inadequate childcare, an inflexible workplace—her return becomes not just challenging but potentially traumatic. Women commonly express surprise—"nobody told me it would be like this"—but rarely admit more difficult truths: that they don't enjoy every moment, that they feel overwhelmed, that they sometimes resent how motherhood has derailed their professional momentum. They are usually silent about it.

This silence isn't accidental. While social media has created space for 'momfluencers' who claim to 'keep it real,' most mothers in everyday life remain hesitant to voice their authentic struggles. Movies like 'Bad Moms' make us laugh because we relate hard. Today's mothers applaud others' honesty while carefully guarding their own complicated feelings, fearing judgement for expressing anything less than maternal bliss. Beyond immediate social consequences lies another concern: what happens when children eventually discover their mothers' honest reflections online? This digital permanence creates yet another invisible rock for mothers to carry.

Derailed Dreams and Delayed Ambitions

Some women I interviewed for this book were brave enough to share raw and honest feelings of motherhood-related resentment anonymously, knowing that it might help other women, but certainly did not ever want their own children to know they felt that way. Most admitted the burden of care in having children was a far bigger impact than they expected, and the physical toll was far higher. The relationship strain was sometimes irreparable and the career disruption catastrophic. I'll note that all of these women love their children. That is not being questioned, or even explored here. It is the disruption to their careers which we explored in our conversation, and the women being able to safely share all feelings about their experiences, even the negative ones, without judgement.

One of these women was Beth (name changed for privacy). With strong aspirations in her teaching career she had set in place a clear path to become a school principal by the age of 30. She then planned to move into public service and politics beyond that. Her dream was to take her real world experience teaching in disadvantaged schools to a public service role informing policy change for widespread social impact. It would have been a noble path. Beth hadn't fully shared her dreams with anyone, riddled with self-doubt and knowing that as a young, country woman, recently married, there were some strong societal expectations around what her next steps should be. Pursuing a political career was not on the menu. Beth's secret desires were swallowed in one gulp with the discovery of an unplanned pregnancy. 'Unplanned pregnancy' is a status you'd normally associate with a single woman, perhaps exploring her sexuality, having some fun, or even being careless with contraception. This was not the case for Beth. She was in her 20's and newly married. It was an expectation held by her family, society, and by her husband, that babies would follow soon after the marriage and establishment of a married household. She was supposed to be happy about it.

At the time, and even now, Beth felt she couldn't disclose the disappointment she felt on finding out she was pregnant. Pregnancy and motherhood were a blessing weren't they? Being a married woman she did not entertain any thoughts there was another option but to go through with the pregnancy and accept her fate. Before the pregnancy, she had negotiated with her husband that they would wait 5 years before they started a family so they could establish careers and be financially secure. Beth was secretly hoping to stretch that out just a bit longer to chase her (unspoken) career dreams. The pregnancy meant that her dreams were pushed aside. She went on to have more children and a successful career in the education sector, but wasn't able to pursue her political dreams.

The timing of motherhood often becomes a critical factor in career trajectory. Whether it arrives unexpectedly early like Beth's, or comes after establishing professional foundations, each woman must navigate the complex intersection of biological reality and professional ambition. The invisible rocks of motherhood weigh differently at various career stages, but they inevitably require women to recalibrate their expectations and priorities.

When Balance Becomes Impossible

Nikki (name changed for privacy) is another woman who spoke about the impact of having children on her career. Her story reveals how motherhood can disrupt even well-established professional rhythms. She explained the disconnect she felt when it was time to return to work after maternity leave with her third child.

Unlike Beth, Nikki had her first two children at the start of her career. She built her professional life and family simultaneously, carefully juggling study, part-time work, and parenthood. By the time she decided to expand their family with a third child, both work and family routines were well established and she was at the point in her job where she was being noticed for potential promotion. This time, stepping away from work to have a baby hit differently. The stakes were higher. With a mortgage, childcare costs, car payments, and the relentless flow of everyday living expenses, the financial pressure was intense.

Inadequate maternity leave provisions forced her back to work far sooner than she would have liked. She returned part-time—a common choice that paradoxically creates more strain, not less. The reduced income stretched the family budget while the compressed schedule left her feeling perpetually behind at work.

This impossible balancing act bred a corrosive sense of inadequacy. Anxiety seeped into both her professional and maternal identities—never feeling fully present or effective in either role. On work days, she mourned missing her children's milestones. On home days, she worried about falling behind on important workplace developments and missing out on advancement opportunities. The psychological toll was relentless.

As burnout crept in, Nikki began recognising the same exhausted resignation in other mothers around her. This recognition sparked a pivotal realisation: her workplace would replace her without hesitation, yet her family could not. She made a conscious decision to redefine her relationship with work—no more long hours, no more sacrificed weekends for a role where she was ultimately replaceable and undervalued.

The revelation wasn't just about workplace demands. It was about the unsustainable combined burden of a demanding career, three children, and the invisible role of being a household manager. The mental load—that constant, invisible work of remembering, planning, and coordinating family life—was crushing. This endless to-do list in her mind included remembering vaccination schedules, planning meals, monitoring clothing sizes, arranging playdates, tracking permission slips, and hundreds of other details that someone in the family must manage. Yet this critical cognitive and emotional work is rarely acknowledged as real work.

Nikki believes that the real impact of motherhood remains dangerously underdiscussed. "Mothers finish their paid work only to go home to what is effectively a second full-time job," she explained. Acknowledging this reality became her first step toward finding a sustainable path forward.

For Nikki, survival depended on two critical supports: colleagues who understood her constraints without judgment, and a community of mothers who validated her experience. This 'village' became her lifeline during the most overwhelming period of her life—a testament to how collective support can help women carry the rocks they cannot put down.

While Nikki's experience highlights the overwhelming pressures of balancing established motherhood with career demands, other women discover that motherhood becomes the lens through which they first truly see workplace gender inequities. Sometimes, it takes experiencing discrimination firsthand to recognise the invisible barriers that were there all along.

Rianne (name changed for privacy) had always considered herself fortunate, even privileged, in her professional life. Before having children, she had never felt denied any opportunities and dismissed the idea that gender inequalities still existed in modern workplaces. Her naivety fuelled her ignorance. "I simply didn't believe women were disadvantaged," she admitted. "If they claimed to be, I assumed it was likely their own choices or actions contributing to the problem." This perspective wasn't merely an abstract opinion—it became the foundation for how she expected her own career to continue uninterrupted after motherhood.

But reality had other plans. As Rianne discovered, her biases would eventually "come back to slap her in the face." In the lead up to her first child, planning for maternity leave meant she was not being included in the more significant and longer term projects. Most organisations would deny this, however, Rianne could see that others were being guided towards the more prestigious projects and promotion opportunities. There were men, certainly, but also women who were not of child-bearing age or stage. Rianne saw the switch as soon as she announced her pregnancy. She became acutely aware of times this had happened to others, but at the time she had been oblivious to the impact of it.

Returning to work after maternity leave, she noticed subtle yet pervasive undercurrents of doubt about her capabilities. Colleagues asked questions about her willingness to travel or work late—questions framed as empathetic concern but rarely directed at new fathers. These seemingly innocuous inquiries revealed the different standards applied to working mothers.

Rianne's first maternity leave concluded with a relatively smooth transition back to work. She attributes this successful return to thoughtful leadership—her senior manager never questioned her capabilities or commitment. This positive experience reinforced her belief that with the right attitude and support, motherhood needn't disrupt career progression.

Her second maternity leave told a different story. While away, significant changes to the company's structure occurred—what businesses call 'organisational restructuring', where roles, reporting lines, and sometimes entire departments are redesigned. This process transformed both her role and the leadership team she'd be working with. Upon returning, Rianne was bluntly informed she had a new position—one she hadn't applied for or been consulted about. The experience created an impossible bind. She had tried to maintain boundaries during her leave—an important psychological separation between work and recovery. Yet this same boundary left her excluded from crucial decisions directly affecting her career. She had departed feeling secure in her expertise and standing within the company, only to return navigating unfamiliar territory while simultaneously managing the intensified home responsibilities of having two small children.

Well-meaning colleagues provided fragments of information about the organisation's changes during her absence, intending to be helpful and keep her in the loop. Instead, these piecemeal updates heightened her anxiety about returning. More destructively, the culture she returned to left her feeling unable to acknowledge she was struggling or being able to request assistance, fearing colleagues would attribute any difficulties to her being a mother who couldn't cope. The unspoken mandate was clear: just get on with it like nothing happened.

Unexpectedly, this challenging experience transformed Rianne into a different kind of leader. In her new high-pressure role, she deliberately modelled healthy boundaries between work and home with her team. She began to recognise how consistently she had deprioritised her own wellbeing when stress mounted, fearing the perception she wasn't measuring up. The cost to her health and relationships had become unsustainable. Rianne began practising what had previously seemed impossible: unapologetic authenticity about her parenting responsibilities. Having a sick child or a sleepless night with a teething toddler became statements of fact rather than sources of guilt or apology. "These aren't circumstances you should feel guilty about or be punished for," she explained. "They're simply the reality of being a parent."

Her deepest insight emerged as she reflected on the stark contrast between her pre-motherhood expectations and the intricate reality she now navigated. The challenges weren't solved merely by having a supportive manager or family help with childcare. The issues were socially imbued and systemic—deeply embedded inequities affecting how both men and women experience parenthood while building careers.

Rianne's perspective had come full circle. The woman who once dismissed gender inequality as exaggerated now advocates for structural changes, particularly for creating opportunities that would allow men greater involvement in early parenting. Her journey from skeptic to advocate reveals how motherhood often reveals invisible systemic barriers that suddenly become impossible to ignore.

While Rianne's journey reveals how motherhood can expose previously invisible gender inequities, not all women experience career disruption with the same sense of injustice. Sometimes, despite far more substantial career interruptions, the emotional response can be strikingly different. The weight of the invisible rocks doesn't always feel like a burden—for some women, it becomes an opportunity for growth, even when the professional sacrifice extends far beyond what they initially anticipated.

Finding Purpose in the Pause

Kate (name changed for privacy), a mother of two, presents a compelling counterpoint to the previous narratives of frustration and constraint. Despite facing a motherhood journey far more challenging than expected, she harbours no resentment for the substantial disruption to her career path.

"My children weren't easy," Kate explained with characteristic directness, "but I wouldn't change a thing." Both of Kate's children are autistic, requiring levels of support and advocacy that removed career advancement from her list of possibilities for much longer than she had ever imagined. Kate had wanted motherhood more than anything else she'd ever wanted, a desire that coloured her response to the challenges that followed. The gratitude she felt for the opportunity to experience motherhood outweighed any professional sacrifices.

Kate's original plan had been modest and conventional—a few years away from work until her youngest settled into pre-school. In theory, this would mean approximately five years as a stay-at-home mum to bond, be present, and lay the foundations for her children's future. Like many women, she assumed she would easily slide back into her career once the early years of sleepless nights, feeding, and nappies were conquered. Reality rewrote this timeline completely. Twelve years passed before Kate could even consider returning to work part-time. Her re-entry faced double constraints: her limited availability was constrained to only include school hours and she also needed the flexibility to leave work at a moment's notice when her children required her support at school.

Remarkably, Kate used this prolonged career pause to complete additional qualifications—a testament to her determination given the already overwhelming demands of raising two high-needs autistic children. This strategic upskilling stemmed from realistic concerns about re-entering her career at entry level, or worse, falling hopelessly behind in her field. By the time she considered returning to the workforce, she was far more qualified than when she left. This professional development, combined with her substantial life experience, gave Kate the confidence to rejoin the workforce as well as advocate for the terms she needed to keep her children's needs at the forefront. Without her dedication to staying connected to her profession through study, she believes she would have felt completely out of her depth navigating industry changes that had evolved during her twelve-year absence.

Kate's re-entry success hinged on finding an employer willing to accommodate her need for flexibility. Beginning in a base-level position that allowed her to continue advocating for her children, she remained with this understanding employer for several years. This arrangement meant she could work without the additional complications of before or after-school care, a crucial consideration for her children's specific needs.

When her marriage ended, financial necessity drove Kate to pursue more substantial income. She developed a newfound hunger for success, rapidly ascending to an executive leadership role. This advancement came with increased demands and a reduction in the flexibility she had relied upon for so long. Remarkably, Kate believes the executive position she now holds is likely where she would have landed regardless. "If my children didn't have additional needs, it probably would have happened much sooner, but the end result is similar." The challenges she navigated made her more resilient and confident—qualities that enabled her to accelerate her career progression despite such a significant gap.

Kate's perspective remains steadfast: she welcomed the opportunity to prioritise her family and feels she has ultimately achieved her professional goals anyway. The journey transformed her leadership style, making her more empathetic and supportive of others facing their own complex circumstances. When asked about what contributed to her success, Kate humbly acknowledged that her own drive had been a crucial factor. Her dedication to hard work and passion for continual learning served as powerful engines for advancement.

Kate's story highlights a critical pattern: too many women fail to credit their own contributions to their success journey. While supportive environments and fortunate circumstances certainly help, ultimately it comes down to personal responsibility in navigating life's unpredictable circumstances. How one chooses to respond to these challenges—whether expected or utterly unforeseen—reveals character and determines forward momentum.

In Kate's case, what might appear as career disruption to outside observers was, in her experience, a different kind of professional development—one that equipped her with rare insights and capabilities that ultimately enhanced her leadership capacity.

The Accumulating Cost of Motherhood

Across these stories of motherhood intersecting with careers—Beth's derailed political aspirations, Nikki's burnout juggling three children and career demands, Rianne's awakening to workplace bias, and Kate's twelve-year career pause—certain patterns emerge with striking clarity. Women consistently accept that motherhood will slow their career progression as though it's an inevitable tax on their gender. They resign themselves to the reality that advancing professionally often means sacrificing the flexibility their caregiver responsibilities demand. Time and again, they justify accepting less professionally with the noble rationale of 'putting family first'.

Choosing to prioritise motherhood over career advancement is entirely valid. The question that lingers, however, is more uncomfortable: how many women would strive for both if our culture didn't relentlessly sell the narrative that motherhood should be fulfilling enough to make up for any professional sacrifices?

Kate's reflections about prioritising her children aren't unique, but the complete absence of resentment stands out as extraordinary. While Kate peacefully accepted career limitations in exchange for the flexibility her autistic children required, most other women I interviewed acknowledged complex feelings about the long-term disadvantages of stepping back during childbearing and child-raising years. These disadvantages are far from temporary or merely emotional. The financial implications of career disruption are concrete and cumulative. Superannuation accounts diminish substantially. The financial implications of career disruption are concrete and cumulative. Consider this: a woman earning $80,000 who takes four years out of the workforce to care for children will lose approximately $280,000 in superannuation by retirement age. This isn't just from the missed employer contributions during those four years (roughly $40,000), but from the decades of compound interest those contributions would have generated. Even when she returns to work, if she shifts to part-time for several years—as many mothers do—the impact multiplies. A woman working three days a week for five years after a full break earns 40% less super than her full-time counterpart. By retirement, the typical Australian woman has about 25% less in her superannuation account than the typical man. These aren't just abstract numbers—they represent real choices women face between being present for bedtime stories and securing their financial future.

Opportunities for promotion and advancement become increasingly distant with each month away from the workplace. This isn't merely about missing specific opportunities during the career pause—it's about a compounding professional penalty that continues decades beyond the actual time away.

Consider how career progression typically works: A woman who takes three to four years away from her career doesn't simply lose three to four years of advancement. She returns to find her peers now three to four levels above her, having accumulated critical experiences, professional relationships, and institutional knowledge she now lacks. Research from the Harvard Business Review shows that women who take career breaks lose an average of 18% of their earning power permanently—not temporarily. Even fifteen years after returning, many women still earn less than counterparts who never left, regardless of comparable skills or performance.

The penalty compounds through what economists call 'opportunity cascades'—each missed promotion means missing the experiences that would qualify you for the next level of advancement.

A woman who returns to work and isn't immediately placed on high-visibility projects misses opportunities to demonstrate leadership, which means she's less likely to be considered for team leadership, which means she's overlooked for departmental leadership, and so on. Like compound interest in reverse, the gap between her career trajectory and her peers' widens exponentially over time.

By the time many women reach their fifties, the accumulation of these diverted opportunities manifests as the 'missing women' phenomenon in executive leadership. A woman who took career breaks in her thirties doesn't just lose those years—she loses the entire alternative career path she might have traveled, along with the financial security, professional recognition, and decision-making influence that would have accompanied it.

The response to these realities takes two distinct forms: some women, like Kate, genuinely recalibrate their career aspirations based on new priorities and values. Others reshape their professional dreams not from authentic preference but to align with society's expectations of maternal sacrifice.

Perhaps most revealing across all interviews was the stark contrast in expectations between mothers and fathers. Without exception, the men who participated in creating these families faced no expectation to step back from their careers when a baby arrived. In fact, they encountered the opposite pressure—to become even more effective breadwinners and career pursuers once parenthood began. The double standard reveals itself most starkly when examining the common social judgements that are attached to motherhood. Women who quickly return to work and outsource childcare and domestic responsibilities face extraordinary criticism. The women I spoke to shared judgemental comments they had faced like "I could never leave my baby that young" and "Why do people have kids they don't want to raise?". Meanwhile, their male partners need only take a few days off for the birth before gliding back to work as though fundamentally unchanged by parenthood. No eyebrows raise when a father misses a school event for work; the same absence by a mother invites scrutiny and judgment.

While women face overt career penalties for motherhood, men encounter a different but equally constraining set of expectations. The pressure on fathers is to pretend that parenthood hasn't affected them professionally at all—a different kind of invisible rock. They're expected to perform at peak capacity despite months of broken sleep during babyhood, with no allowance for the cognitive and emotional impacts of new parenthood.

These expectations rarely align with what many men actually anticipated fatherhood would be like. Many modern fathers want deeper involvement with their children's daily lives but find themselves trapped in workplace cultures that penalise such engagement. This misalignment creates its own form of silent suffering—a father physically present at work but emotionally pulled toward home. This rigid framework for fatherhood inadvertently compounds the burdens placed on mothers. When workplace cultures prevent men from sharing family responsibilities, women inherit them by default. This arrangement creates a perfect recipe for relationship resentment, with neither partner able to fully inhabit their desired roles within the family they are creating. They are expected to accept the roles society has created.

Acceptance is not resignation; it's a powerful catalyst for change. Some of the women I interviewed have embraced their circumstances without surrendering to them. They've acknowledged the challenges they've faced and integrated their new 'normal' into reconstructed identities that honour both their professional ambitions and their maternal experiences. Through this genuine acceptance—not of gender inequity, but of their own complex journeys—these women have discovered newfound strength. For some, like Kate, this meant paving the way for a triumphant professional return after years of focused parenting. For others, it meant finding peace in choices that prioritised wellbeing and balance over conventional success metrics.

Their stories collectively echo a powerful sentiment: acknowledging our values, vulnerabilities and limitations often becomes the first step toward rebuilding and reclaiming our lives, especially when those lives diverge dramatically from our original plans. This acknowledgment doesn't mean surrendering ambition—rather, it creates space for more authentic and sustainable success.

The women profiled here demonstrate that career disruption, while challenging, can also become a crucible for developing rare and valuable capabilities. Their experiences of navigating these complex territories—often without maps or guides—have equipped them with resilience, perspective, and leadership qualities that might otherwise have remained undeveloped.

While acceptance has provided some women a path to reclaiming their professional identities, other women's journeys reveal how motherhood can trigger a series of cascading disruptions—each adaptation leading to another unexpected turn. For these women, career disruption isn't a single event but a recurring pattern that follows them across time and even geography. Their stories demonstrate how even the most promising arrangements can unravel when family needs shift, creating ripple effects that extend far beyond the initial pause.

The mothers in these stories aren't asking for their rocks to disappear—many of these responsibilities are central to their identities and values. What they seek is acknowledgment of the weight, flexibility in how they carry it, and occasional offers of sharing the load. Mostly, they want recognition that carrying these rocks isn't a personal challenge to be overcome through individual grit, but a systemic distribution of weight that could be balanced more equitably.

Motherhood stands apart as perhaps the heaviest and most transformative load many women will carry. It reshapes not just careers but identities, priorities, and perspectives. The resilience these women demonstrate isn't just about perseverance—it's about the remarkable human capacity to adapt, reinvent, and find meaning even when the path looks nothing like what was originally envisioned. They carry their rocks not because they have no choice, but because they continuously choose what matters most to them, even when those choices come with significant professional consequences.

Detour Through Devastation

Facing Mortality

Life's obstacle course inevitably includes passages through darkness. While motherhood represents a predictable—albeit challenging—career detour that many women consciously choose, there are other detours that arrive without warning, redirecting professional paths with devastating swiftness.

When grief, illness, and survival become part of a woman's journey, the invisible rocks she carries transform dramatically. The weight and grief of loss, the physical burden of illness, the psychological load of confronting mortality—these rocks aren't just heavy; they're transformative. They change not only how a woman navigates her career, but how she understands her place in the world.

Unlike the motherhood detour, which society at least acknowledges (however inadequately), these detours through grief and illness often remain unspoken in professional contexts. There are no "congratulations" cards or structured leave policies for a cancer diagnosis. Few workplace conversations accommodate the reality that a bereaved colleague may function at reduced capacity for years, not days or weeks. The invisibility of these particular rocks becomes especially acute when women must carry them alone, without established cultural scripts for integrating such significant disruptions into professional identities.

The women whose stories fill this chapter have navigated terrain no career planning workshop could possibly prepare you for. They've rewritten their own professional narratives while confronting serious illness, or rebuilt lives shattered by sudden tragedy. Their invisible rocks aren't the expected weights of gendered expectations or caregiving responsibilities, but the existential burdens that come when death enters the equation—either as immediate reality or looming possibility.

These stories reveal how women's careers can be irrevocably altered by encounters with loss and illness, creating detours that lead to entirely different destinations than originally planned. Yet they also demonstrate the extraordinary capacity for resilience, reinvention, and meaning-making that emerges when women navigate these most difficult passages of human experience.

Amber (name changed for privacy), an ambitious and successful Assistant Principal, was faced with the sudden and unexpected loss of her husband while in her twenties—a detour no career plan includes, carrying rocks no professional development prepares you for. Her career journey had begun promisingly. As a young graduate teacher, Amber accepted a position in Sydney's inner west. She had barely twenty-four hours to decide, but decided the adventure was worth pursuing. She and her boyfriend (later husband) left their coastal hometown ready to build their future in the big city. Over four years, she flourished professionally, steadily accumulating leadership responsibilities and experience.

Despite professional success, city life never quite fit their vision for the future. Amber and her husband began looking toward regional communities that aligned with their long term lifestyle aspirations. When Amber interviewed for a permanent role at a small country school, she felt an immediate connection—not just to the position, but to the rural life it represented. Though disappointed to narrowly miss out, her potential hadn't gone unnoticed. The principal offered her a two-year contract shortly afterwards as Assistant Principal. This was enough incentive for the couple to have a go at country living.

With Amber's career flourishing and their new lifestyle taking shape, everything seemed to be falling into place. Beneath this professional momentum, her husband's health was deteriorating. He had gastric sleeve surgery to address weight-related issues, but suddenly began experiencing unexplained seizures just ten days post-procedure. These episodes initially occurred every few weeks, often while he was sleeping.

The reality of regional healthcare quickly tarnished their country dream. Securing a neurologist appointment meant months of waiting, extensive travel, accommodation costs, and time away from work. The disconnected nature of rural medical services demanded constant self-advocacy, creating an additional invisible burden Amber carried alongside her professional duties. As the seizures intensified and became more frequent, Amber found herself taking unplanned time off work—a particular challenge in her leadership role, where her absence undermined her ability to provide consistent leadership to her team. The unpredictability of her husband's condition meant yet another rock added to her already heavy load.

The devastating turn came without warning. After yet another seizure at work—something that had become almost routine—her husband's colleague helped him home, where he went to bed expecting to recover as usual. But that night, Amber woke to find him experiencing a seizure far more severe than any before. He fell between the bed and bedside table, his large frame making it impossible for her to move him to safety as the seizure violently intensified. When he became unresponsive, Amber called emergency services and enlisted a neighbour's help to move him. She performed CPR under the guidance of operators until paramedics arrived. Though the preceding events remain etched in vivid detail in her memory, what followed became a blur. All she remembers once the paramedics arrived is they took her husband away. Amber's husband never returned.

Workplace responses to personal loss reveals how ill-equipped our professional structures are to accommodate grief. Amber had accumulated seven weeks of leave, barely enough to cover a school term. In comparison, many organisations offer drastically inadequate bereavement provisions—often a single day for immediate family—raising the impossible question: How is anyone supposed to return to full function days after losing someone they love?

Amber's eventual return to work was fragmented by psychological appointments and unexpected waves of intense grief. Her career progression stalled completely as she functioned well below her capacity. It took a long time before she felt any sense of forward movement, professionally or personally.

While supportive leadership and patience contributed to her healing, Amber also found purpose in sharing her story and advocating for improved rural health access. The career detour forced upon her by grief eventually led to a different kind of identity—one that incorporated her loss rather than merely working around it or moving past it.

When Illness Chooses the Path

While the loss of a loved one envelops us with grief and uncertainty, another impactful detour occurs when a person's own mortality enters the equation. The invisible rocks of serious illness carry a different weight—one that forces women to navigate not just external loss, but fundamental questions about identity, capability, and future possibility. The next story reveals how a cancer diagnosis created its own permanent detour, one that altered her professional trajectory even decades after recovery.

Not all disruptions are recoverable. Hannah (name changed for privacy) reveals that even fifteen years after her cancer diagnosis, she has never been able to properly re-establish her career. Her story illuminates how illness doesn't merely pause professional momentum—it can permanently alter a woman's relationship with her own capabilities and aspirations.

Hannah had been thriving in middle management with a clear path to senior leadership, what she describes as "the pinnacle of her career." At the height of her professional prowess, Hannah could see the rewards for years of dedicated work finally within reach. Her professional success was mirrored in her personal life—family relationships, social connections, and physical wellbeing all seemed perfectly aligned. She embodied the fulfilled, high-achieving, professional woman.

This harmonious life began unravelling after a routine yoga class when Hannah discovered a lump under her arm. Like many women accustomed to prioritising others and not themselves, she was tempted to dismiss it due to being too busy with work and family. Only a casual mention to her mother—who insisted she seek medical attention—set her on a different path. Within twenty-four hours of her initial consultation, Hannah faced the shocking reality of urgent surgery.

Her life's momentum was abruptly redirected into an endless cycle of waiting rooms, medical appointments, tests, and treatments. Grueling chemotherapy and painful breast reconstruction surgery transformed her physically and psychologically. A super-fit and high-performing, mid-life, inner-city professional became someone who could barely manage a short walk to the local coffee shop. Even then only under her retired mother's supervision.

Hannah's workplace held her position for a year—a gesture that she was grateful for. It made her feel supported and valued. She desperately wanted to reclaim her former life, to return to the career that had defined her identity and had showcased her capabilities. It was a job that really brought out the best in her. She wanted things to go back to normal.

Just three days after attempting to return once she was medically given the 'all clear', the devastating truth became unavoidable: she could no longer perform at management level. Chronic fatigue, severe brain fog—that frustrating cognitive cloudiness that made concentrating, remembering details, and processing information nearly impossible—and shattered confidence made her previous role untenable. Where Hannah had once effortlessly juggled multiple complex projects, she now struggled to follow a single conversation without losing her train of thought. Once-simple tasks like participating in meetings or making quick decisions had become exhausting challenges.

The decision to resign came from both self-protection and a sense of professional integrity. Holding a position she couldn't effectively perform in seemed unfair to the organisation she had served so diligently, and had been so fair to her. Hannah's employer, recognising the value of her experience despite her diminished capacity, offered her casual work at a lower level. This arrangement allowed Hannah to maintain some professional identity while adjusting expectations about her capabilities.

Hannah clung to the hope that this diminished capacity was temporary—that eventually she would return to high-performance mode and reclaim her interrupted career trajectory. She even relocated to a warmer climate and prioritised wellbeing, making all the 'right' choices for recovery. Yet despite being medically recovered from cancer and living an enviably healthy lifestyle, her confidence and energy remained shattered. Even as she was able to work more hours, she consistently held herself back from leadership opportunities and responsibility-laden projects, having internalised her limitations as permanent truths. Self-doubt became fact; her lingering symptoms became proof, to Hannah, of her diminished value.

Eventually, Hannah moved again to be closer to her family and found what she calls her "dream job for that period". It was a position calibrated perfectly to her post-illness reality. It offered just enough challenge to utilise her skills without overwhelming her fragile reserves. This carefully balanced arrangement provided several years of stability. It all fell apart when new leadership brought toxicity to her workplace.

What should have been Hannah's final professional chapter before retirement instead reopened wounds she thought had healed and scarred over. Being micromanaged and undermined reactivated the insecurities her illness had planted years before. Hannah had dramatically underestimated how close to the surface these old wounds remained. She took a long time to realise how easily a different kind of workplace disruption could trigger the same sense of inadequacy and inferiority that her cancer had first introduced into her professional identity. For someone who knew in her heart and soul that she was strong and resilient, she suddenly wasn't either of those things.

Hannah's story reveals the insidious long-term impact of serious illness on women's careers. The visible disruption—treatment, recovery, physical limitations—eventually ends. The invisible rocks remain: diminished confidence, recalibrated expectations, and a fundamentally altered relationship with professional ambition. These lasting effects create a career detour from which there is often no complete return to the original path.

Hannah's career detour began with sudden illness disrupting her professional momentum, and then re-emerged as trauma in later experiences, reminding her of the immense weight of her invisible rocks. Some women navigate multiple, sequential redirections that compound and intersect in complex ways. The rocks we carry aren't always added one at a time—sometimes life hands over several at once, or introduces new burdens just as we think others are finally set down. Career detours often appear just when we believe the path has finally straightened and we've started to relax. It almost makes us not want to feel secure, and not relax, because that's when the ground beneath our feet shifts again.

Intersecting Detours

Someone else who understands the ripple effects of a cancer diagnosis is Jillian (name changed for privacy). Her experience reveals how illness can turn up out of nowhere and how what you prioritise plays a big part in how you face the challenges in front of you. Jillian's first significant career disruption was entirely welcome—motherhood. Unlike many women who feel pressured to minimise their professional pause for children, she embraced her maternal identity wholeheartedly. People kept asking when she would return to work, but the truth was, she didn't want to. She wanted to be a mum. Jillian spent ten years fully focused on raising her children before feeling any desire to re-enter the workforce.

Her eventual return began cautiously with part-time work. However, with shortages of staff in her industry, she was quickly pulled into full-time work. The transition proved challenging. During her first year back, Jillian attributed her struggle with the excessive workload to her own rusty skills and outdated knowledge. She assumed the difficulties would diminish as she updated her industry familiarity and reacclimated to professional demands. Three to four years into her return, a more sobering realisation emerged. The job wasn't getting easier—it was getting harder. The problem wasn't her decade-long absence but the nature of the profession itself. During her time away, her profession had become increasingly demanding and unsustainable.

The turning point came when Jillian recognised how her professional exhaustion was spilling into her family life. She found herself emotionally unavailable to her children—switching off during conversations and failing to be present in ways she valued. Even simple questions like "How was your day?" became sources of distress, forcing her to mentally relive workplace challenges and preventing any meaningful separation between professional and personal life.

This recognition brought substantial regret. Jillian lamented not having sufficient "space in her mind" for her own children during those intense working years. When she asked her children for feedback about her full-time work schedule, their negative responses confirmed what she already felt—something needed to change. Jillian transitioned to casual employment, which restored precious balance to her life. With this newfound equilibrium, she and her husband began planning to reconnect through travel, though her primary goal was to reclaim her maternal presence.

Just as this more sustainable life chapter was taking shape, Jillian scheduled a routine mammogram. It was a basic health maintenance task she'd been 'too busy' to complete during her full-time working years. This seemingly simple act of self-care led to a devastating discovery: Stage 1 cancer.

The diagnosis prompted unsettling retrospection. Jillian often wondered whether the intense stress of those overwhelming years balancing work and motherhood had contributed to her cancer susceptibility. Even more disturbing was the realisation that had she continued working full-time, she might have postponed the mammogram indefinitely, potentially allowing the cancer to advance undetected. Despite having no symptoms, the disease had already established itself in her body, and the thought of how far it might have progressed without early detection remains deeply troubling to her.

Jillian recalls her naïveté following the initial mammogram. When called back for additional tests, she sensed something was wrong but dismissed her fears. Even as the receptionist described special parking arrangements and advised bringing snacks and reading material for the extended testing process, Jillian clung to optimism. She made the two-hour journey alone, certain a support person was unnecessary.

Protecting her family from worry, Jillian minimised the situation when telling them about it. She mentioned needing a biopsy without elaborating, later wondering why nobody recognised this the red flag she herself had downplayed. Her family shared her innocent assumption that nothing serious could be wrong. After all, she was only in her early forties, appeared healthy, and had no symptoms.

The moment of receiving confirmation remains etched in her memory—particularly telling her husband and watching him struggle to maintain composure while processing the news. Their travel plans were immediately suspended, their future suddenly restructured around the all-consuming routine of chemotherapy and medical appointments.

When we spoke, Jillian was in recovery and preparing to return to casual work. Her confidence about this return was fragile. She worried about how colleagues and clients would respond to her physical transformation—the greying pixie cut, recognised universally by survivors, that had replaced her pre-chemotherapy hair. Working with vulnerable people, she feared her cancer story might trigger distress in those who had lost loved ones to the disease or create unnecessary anxiety for people already carrying too many burdens. This final concern encapsulates a pattern that appears throughout so many women's career detours: even amid personal crisis, women often place others' needs before their own. Jillian's worry about how her illness might affect other people's emotional wellbeing, rather than focusing exclusively on her own recovery, demonstrates how the rocks of caregiving remain firmly in women's arms even when the woman thinks she has put some of them down.

Jillian's journey illustrates how career detours rarely occur in isolation. Her story weaves together the motherhood detour, which she embraced as a positive choice, with an unexpected illness. She wasn't even sick. This detour intruded just as she had found a sustainable balance. These intersecting disruptions created a unique career path shaped by sequential adaptations, each requiring different forms of resilience and reinvention. Unlike the motherhood detour, which society at least acknowledges (however inadequately), these detours through grief and illness often remain unspoken in professional contexts. There are no "congratulations" cards or structured leave policies for a cancer diagnosis. Few workplace conversations accommodate the reality that a bereaved colleague may function at reduced capacity for years, not days or weeks. The invisibility of these particular rocks becomes especially acute when women must carry them without established cultural scripts for integrating such devastating disruptions into professional identities. These scripts are the shared social understandings and expected behaviors that guide us through major life transitions. While we have recognised patterns for announcing pregnancies at work, returning from parental leave, or even celebrating retirement, there are no established protocols for saying "I have cancer" to colleagues or returning to work after losing a spouse. Society lacks shared language and rituals to help navigate these territories, leaving women to improvise their way through terrain that remains unfamiliar in professional settings. And frankly, it shouldn't be this way. The commonality of the experience should make it something that is prepared for, not something we pretend won't happen.

Recalibrating your Professional Compass

The stories of Amber, Hannah, and Jillian uncover a fundamental truth about career disruption: when death enters the equation—either as an immediate reality or confronted possibility—the invisible rocks women carry transform in both weight and meaning. These are not the the same as the expected burdens of gender expectations or the anticipated challenges of motherhood, but existential weights that fundamentally alter how women view themselves, their capabilities, and their professional futures.

Amber's sudden widowhood thrust her into uncharted professional territory. The shock of losing her partner while holding a demanding leadership role brought to light the impossible expectation that personal devastation can be compartmentalised away from professional responsibilities.

Hannah's cancer diagnosis derailed what had been a carefully constructed career trajectory. Her story illustrates how serious illness doesn't just interrupt work—it fundamentally alters cognitive capacity, confidence, and professional identity. The assumption that medical recovery equals readiness to resume previous roles ignores the complex psychological rebuilding required.

Jillian's diagnosis arrived precisely when she had achieved the balance she sought between motherhood and career. Her journey demonstrates how life can change direction suddenly, and often just as women believe they've finally found sustainable equilibrium, forcing them to reconstruct their professional and personal lives yet again while managing treatment and recovery.

Each of these experiences represents a different facet of how encounters with mortality reshape professional identity. Unlike the motherhood detour, which society at least acknowledges (however inadequately), these journeys through grief and significant illness remain largely hidden from view in professional contexts. Bereavement leave policies expect recovery in days. Workplaces expect that cancer survivors return unchanged. The unspoken pressure is there to keep personal tragedy separate from professional performance. This reflects how poorly most work structures accommodate these formative life experiences.

Where women once defined themselves by achievement, advancement, or expertise, their harrowing experiences have shifted their focus to different values and capabilities. Amber's advocacy for rural healthcare access, Hannah's reluctant acceptance of diminished capacity, and Jillian's heightened awareness of balance represent not merely adaptations but transformations in how these women understand their purpose in work. The question shifts from "How can I advance my career?" to deeper inquiries: "What work matters given my new understanding of life's fragility?" and "How can my experiences serve others?" Their professional compasses are permanently reset, pointing toward new destinations they never intended to seek.

There is no end to the ebb and flow of joy and sadness in the world. Everyone will inevitably experience both ends of this spectrum and everything in between. There is no way to measure grief, adversity, and strength on the same scale, and there is absolute inequity in the distribution of hardship. The rocks some women are handed weigh heavier than others, appear at different moments in their journey, and must be carried for varying distances.

These experiences didn't just derail careers—they fundamentally transformed what professional fulfillment could look like. The women found themselves not just facing new challenges, but operating in an entirely different professional reality.

Finding joy in the tatters of what was once a carefully planned life requires a resilience rarely acknowledged in training or workshops. It demands the courage to rebuild not just careers but entire identities, often without clear models or established paths. The women in these stories demonstrate that carrying the heaviest rocks builds more than strength. It builds wisdom, perspective, and a deep understanding of what truly matters—insights that transform how they approach both work and life.

The Karmic Detour

An Unpredictable Path

Some career detours don't announce themselves with clear signposts. They creep in through toxic workplace cultures or accumulate through personal crises, gradually obscuring the path forward and challenging everything women understand about professional identity.

Good times and bad times happen to everyone, but good luck and bad luck is not distributed fairly/ Some people get more misfortune raining upon them in a month than others get in a lifetime. I used to believe in karma—that fairness would eventually prevail, that those causing harm would face consequences, and that good intentions would be rewarded. I was wrong. Karma is a fickle and unreliable acquaintance who can't be trusted to deliver justice.

It's easy to put your faith in Karma—I certainly have. You nurture this relationship, expecting fairness and justice in return. But Karma is a false friend who sets the terms and breaks them at will. Karma is the colleague who smiles while undermining you, the boss who promises promotion while planning your redundancy. Instead of delivering justice to bullies, Karma punishes those brave enough to speak up.

There's a good chance that Karma is a narcissistic psychopath causing grief and turmoil just for fun, just throwing in the occasional good thing as a public relations manoeuvre.

The downside of Karma's unreliability is that doing good things does not improve the chances that good will happen to you. On the plus side of this disappointment is when things are tough, remarkable women emerge with levels of resilience and volition that rock the earth to its core.

When women face toxic workplaces or compounding personal crises, they're forced onto detours they could never anticipate. These aren't the culturally recognised detours of motherhood or the sympathetically understood journeys through loss and illness. These are chaotic redirections that arrive when life and work seem to conspire against you. Karma offers no rescue.

The invisible rocks these women carry aren't just heavy—they're corrosive. They're the weight of gaslighting, of having legitimate concerns dismissed as overreactions, of being told to "toughen up" while drowning. They're the exhausting burden of maintaining professional composure while your personal world collapses behind a false facade.

These are the women who are dealt the worst cards imaginable, but still manage to stay in the game, kick ass, and sometimes even win. There are women who face it head-on, side-on and from below. Their stories are not about the size of the hurdles they encountered or the enormity of the obstacles they overcame but about the strength they discovered within themselves. These are the women who embody resilience—rising from the ashes, ready to rewrite their stories and redefine success on their own terms.

Fuck Karma, it's women who deserve to be worshipped.

Karma's Betrayal

When we talk about unfair distribution of hardship, some women seem to have Karma actively working against them, piling crisis upon crisis until the weight becomes almost unbearable. These women embody the resilience that emerges not by choice, but by brutal necessity. Their career detours aren't always caused by a single catastrophic event, but by an avalanche of personal crises that make professional aspirations feel like a luxury they can no longer afford.

Rachel (name changed for privacy) exemplifies this relentless accumulation of bad luck. Her career detour began with a cascade of family medical emergencies that defied any sense of fairness or karmic balance. Rachel's world began unraveling when her son discovered a mysterious lump on his leg. The diagnosis—a rare cancerous lymphoma requiring urgent surgery with the risk of amputation—pushed everything else from her mind. But Rachel already had plenty of 'everything else' weighing on her.

Her husband had been experiencing dramatic personality changes that were tearing their marriage apart. What she didn't know then was that his erratic behavior stemmed from a serious medical condition affecting his cognition. The neurological symptoms, personality shifts, and relationship strain were all connected, but at the time, the marriage felt like it was simply disintegrating.

The moment her son's diagnosis came through, everything else became secondary. Rachel packed her bags, took unpaid leave, and relocated to a city hours from home to support her son through surgery and recovery. COVID lockdowns made the situation even more challenging—she couldn't travel back and forth between the country hospital and home, so she committed to months away while her husband's condition remained undiagnosed and untreated.

Fortunately, her son emerged cancer-free, but Rachel's relief was short-lived. While she'd been away caring for him, her husband's condition had deteriorated significantly. When a diagnosis finally emerged months later, it placed him on a transplant waiting list and landed him in ICU for weeks. Once again, Rachel took unpaid leave and relocated to support him through another life-threatening crisis.

She remained torn about their relationship. She was uncertain whether his health issues alone had damaged their marriage or if the problems ran deeper. Despite her doubts about their future together, she stood by his side as he received a successful transplant and a second chance at life.

Just as Rachel dared to hope the worst was behind them—her son cancer-free, her husband recovering—tragedy struck again. A young family member died suddenly, shaking the entire family to its core. The grief, fear, and turmoil that Rachel had been suppressing throughout months of crisis finally erupted. All the emotions she hadn't had time to process while focused on everyone else's survival came flooding back with devastating force.

Compound trauma isn't just multiple difficult experiences—it's a web of interconnected wounds where each new crisis reactivates previous unhealed injuries. Unlike single-incident trauma, these experiences create psychological impacts greater than their individual parts, overwhelming the mind's protective mechanisms. The brain's protective mechanisms become overwhelmed trying to process multiple threats simultaneously. This creates symptoms that don't follow predictable patterns of recovery. For Rachel, her son's cancer, husband's illness, and loss of a family member weren't experienced as separate events with clear beginnings and endings, but as a continuous landscape where healing from one crisis was interrupted by the emergence of the next.

Combine this with resilience fatigue—that state of emotional and psychological exhaustion that comes when someone has been strong for too long, drawing from the same well of coping resources without time to replenish them—and you begin to understand Rachel's state of mind. Tired. Tired of feeling, thinking, trying to understand and tired of being strong. Unlike ordinary fatigue that follows a single difficult event and resolves with rest, resilience fatigue accumulates across multiple challenges, gradually depleting a person's capacity to bounce back until even small setbacks feel insurmountable. It's the emotional equivalent of running multiple marathons back-to-back without recovery time between races.

When Rachel reflected on what got her through this horrific time, she believed it was because she had no choice. She explained that she simply had to get up each day and go through the motions. People were depending on her. It took a couple of years before the enormity of enduring trauma after trauma finally hit her. She held herself together through the parts where her son needed her—nothing in life comes close to a mother's love for her child. She didn't allow any of the experience to be about her or what she might need as support. It was all about her child.

Beyond that, she didn't feel like she was holding anything together at all. She had the strength to do the mothering, but felt completely overwhelmed by everything else. She wasn't sleeping. She was unwell. Returning to work became impossible.

Rachel's career became collateral damage in this series of personal catastrophes. The unpaid leave, the geographic displacement, the emotional exhaustion—each crisis demanded pieces of her professional identity until work became merely background noise rather than a core part of who she was. This is one way personal trauma creates professional detours: not by choice, but by the crushing weight of survival needs that make career engagement feel trivial by comparison.

The Human Face of Workplace Cruelty

While Rachel's career detour was forced by external family crises, other women find their professional paths derailed from within the workplace itself. Where Rachel faced the unfair distribution of life's traumatic experiences that spilled over into her work, other women encounter Karma's injustice in a different form—when toxic colleagues or managers become the direct source of trauma, transforming perfectly good workplaces into hell on earth for those in their orbit. In these cases, the career detour isn't created by external circumstances, but from within.

Sue (name changed for privacy) had been an educational leader for many years, passionate about equity and opportunity for students who didn't fit conventional moulds. Once, when she found herself working under a new manager, the relationship got off to a deeply troubling start: she had to tell him to address her face, not her chest, during conversations. The fact that she needed to say "my eyes are up here" to a professional colleague set the tone for what would become her first toxic working relationship and made her far more aware and empathetic to workplace dynamics. She saw herself as a person who championed fairness and equity for staff in the workplace, not afraid to call people out on inappropriate jokes and comments.

Sue knew she was right to speak up, but couldn't navigate the relationship with this boss afterward due to the imbalance of power. She knew that keeping her mouth shut would have secured her another contract, but she chose her own integrity instead, leaving the job and moving on to different opportunities. Women are more commonly in insecure contract roles—especially when returning from parental leave—leaving them without a secure foundation from which to defend their rights.

After a few short-term contracts, Sue landed an exciting leadership role which had close alignment with her passions for working with disadvantaged youth. She enjoyed the work and loved the people she worked with. It seemed like the perfect career redemption after her experience with the sexist manager—until this new professional sanctuary became tarnished by someone she describes as a "psychopath."

Sue is now on leave with a diagnosed psychological injury—formal recognition that workplace conditions have caused measurable harm to her mental health requiring medical intervention and rehabilitation—Sue works with medical professionals on a recovery she never expected to need. Unlike physical workplace injuries that are immediately visible and rarely questioned, psychological injuries often face skepticism despite being equally legitimate and potentially more debilitating. In Australia and some other countries, these injuries are recognized by workers' compensation systems, though proving them typically requires extensive documentation, multiple medical opinions, and a willingness to have one's mental health scrutinized in ways physical injuries rarely are.

Perhaps the most devastating aspect for Sue isn't the injury itself, but the realisation that another human being deliberately caused it. Sue had always seen herself as a strong, confident woman who advocated fearlessly for herself and others. Having a workplace colleague diminish her to the point of professional dysfunction wrapped her in layers of embarrassment and shame she struggles to articulate.

What makes this situation interesting is that, unlike her previous experience with the sexist manager, no clear power imbalance existed. Her tormentor held no formal authority and occupied a lower-ranking role, exposing the uncomfortable truth that toxicity doesn't require positional power to destroy someone's professional wellbeing.

When Sue finally acknowledged the damage, she began methodically collecting evidence and documenting the behavior. The process of documentation—intended to protect herself—became its own form of trauma. Putting forth her complaint, collating evidence, and working with psychologists proved highly retraumatising, forcing her to repeatedly relive the harm while feeling that others questioned her recollections and reliability. It left her questioning her own reliability. This secondary trauma explains why many people ultimately walk away from toxic workplace situations rather than speak up—the systems designed to address psychological harm often inflict additional damage.

The psychological impact has been enormous, making Sue question herself, her values, her skills, and her future. She describes the dark periods as waves—unpredictable and overwhelming. What makes this loss particularly cruel is that Sue had finally found what many women spend their entire careers seeking: a workplace that felt like a perfect fit, a professional space where she truly belonged. That sense of belonging was methodically destroyed through the calculated manipulation of a single person. The tactics themselves sound almost trivial when listed individually—important information withheld, rumors spread, alliances built against her. It resembles schoolyard behavior, which is precisely why Sue initially dismissed it as imagination or low-level workplace drama from an insecure colleague.

Sue's experience resonates with me on a deeply personal level. I've also had to come to terms with being eroded in ways that surprised me. For me, it came in the form of multiple poorly managed changes. There were three major organisational restructures plus several smaller reshuffles in my department in just a few short years. During one restructure alone, more than 100 people lost their jobs. While some changes seemed logical, the processes were poorly handled and compromised everyone's wellbeing. It felt like senior leaders were playing games of power with little consideration for the humans that were being impacted.

My story can be distilled to this: new leadership swooped in with a vision for short-term gains at the expense of the longer-term projects I was involved with. For months, I struggled to understand why every initiative from my department met resistance. Projects that once moved smoothly were suddenly blocked. Innovative thinking from my portfolio was being dismissed. Proposals disappeared into administrative black holes. Training opportunities for my team were even being withheld and I couldn't work out why. I've never worked so hard and was close to burnout. The red-tape and roadblocks I encountered was baffling—until the truth eventually emerged.

Meanwhile, my team operated under constant uncertainty. As their leader, I felt responsible for their wellbeing as rumours circulated about our programs' future. When senior leadership finally shared their vision—with deliberately vague details, and delivered a week before Christmas—the timing and lack of clarity only served to intensify everyone's anxiety.

The full impact remained hidden until five months later, when the official details were released. Only then did I learn the truth: my position was being eliminated entirely and the funding from our programs that connected disadvantaged regional and rural communities with higher education was being redirected into other areas. I had spent months advocating for my team's job security and had neglected to advocate for my own role. I had expected changes to my responsibilities—not complete elimination of the role. I came to understand that none of us truly matter in any workplace. We are all highly replaceable. My own insignificance came and smacked me in the face.

My passion for regional education and equity came from my lived experience. As a teen mum from a small town who used education and motivation to challenge stereotypes and break free from expectations, the job had felt like a perfect alignment of my values and skills: creating pathways to higher education that could change life trajectories. This felt like so much more than just a job for me. I was passionate and dedicated. It was a large part of my identity.

When you're suddenly deemed unnecessary in your workplace, your professional confidence doesn't just waver—it collapses. "This is not personal, it's about the organisation," they insisted. But that explanation did nothing to soften the deeply personal impact. The relationship of trust and loyalty I believed existed had been an illusion.

In the aftermath, I questioned everything. Had the work I'd poured my heart into actually mattered? Had I overestimated my own value? My professional identity unraveled completely. I was devastated—and then even more devastated about being so devastated! My logical inner voice kept saying "It's just a job," but if it was truly just a job, why did losing it hurt so much? What was wrong with me?

I wanted answers immediately. But I was also tired. So, so tired from months of upheaval, loss, and grief. Where was Karma now? Where was the justice for those who had been harmed? Karma remained conspicuously absent when I needed her most. Like Sue, I discovered that workplace toxicity doesn't just create a career detour—it forces a complete recalibration of who you believe yourself to be, while Karma sits on the sidelines, indifferent to our suffering.

Workplace Battlegrounds

Many people I've spoken to about toxic workplace disruptions carry the trauma in their giant bag of invisible rocks long into their futures. They try to dismiss their grief and trauma (myself included), but eventually face triggers that force them to confront it. The dismissal becomes a coping strategy—they convince themselves the experience was partly their fault, not really that bad, or just how every workplace operates. This self-gaslighting protects them temporarily but doesn't heal the wound.

Poor organisational change is recognised in Australia as a psychosocial hazard, that is, something that is identified as being a potential source of mental and emotional harm, but organisations have a long way to go in protecting the human beings in their charge. Some first steps would include making organisations accountable for the psychological damage they inflict on employees during times of change, and during changes in leadership or direction.

Many people encounter workplace incivility, another recognised psychosocial hazard that creates risk of harm when left unaddressed. Employees who speak up often have their concerns dismissed, downplayed, or disregarded by human resource (HR) departments focused on managing organisational risk rather than protecting people.

HR frequently serves power-hungry leaders willing to cover their own transgressions rather than supporting employees who raise legitimate concerns.

This is why trauma-informed approaches to handling complaints are crucial in workplaces. A trauma-informed approach recognises that many people have experienced trauma and understands how it affects behavior, decision-making, and coping mechanisms. Rather than asking "What's wrong with you?" it asks "What happened to you?" and responds with safety, trustworthiness, and collaboration rather than judgement. You never know what others have experienced in their work and personal lives. Having empathy, flexibility, and supportive systems in place goes a long way toward protecting those who have experienced workplace toxicity or personal trauma. Trust takes years to build and milliseconds to destroy. Someone like Rachel, who is carrying the trauma from consecutive events, or someone like Sue who is going to be afraid to trust her relationships with colleagues, will need compassion and sensitivity to feel safe in future workplaces.

Sometimes workplace toxicity isn't from a single narcissistic individual, but from systems and cultures that have normalised cruelty under the guise of professionalism. Recently, I met a woman whose story exemplifies this systemic and cultural callousness.

A couple of months after her daughter died, Peta (name changed for privacy) returned to work, hoping routine would provide some stability amidst her grief. Instead of support, she was chastised by management for "not being as talkative" as before. When she cried at work in front of clients on what would have been her daughter's birthday, she wasn't met with compassion—she was pulled into a disciplinary meeting and told to "rein it in."

The organisation's message was unmistakable: her grief was inconvenient and seen as unprofessional. Her humanity was seen as an impediment to workplace efficiency. Other grief-related behaviors—arriving late one day, eating lunch alone, struggling to concentrate and even asking for help—were systematically documented as performance issues. She watched helplessly as management built a case against her, transforming her natural responses to devastating loss into grounds for termination.

This experience represents perhaps the most egregious form of the toxic detour—when workplaces not only fail to support women through life's most devastating challenges but actively punish them for their natural human responses. It reflects an organisational culture where emotional authenticity is treated as a liability rather than recognised as part of our shared humanity. This is backed by systems and processes which allow such a cruel approach to occur.

A toxic detour isn't just about the career interruption it creates— it's about the fundamental violation of women's sense of self when their legitimate experiences and emotions are invalidated, minimised, or weaponised against them. Whether it's Rachel navigating multiple crises, Sue confronting workplace psychological abuse, my own experience of organisational betrayal, or Peta, a bereaved mother being disciplined for grieving, the pattern remains consistent: women are expected to carry their invisible rocks without acknowledgment, without support, and without the rocks ever affecting their performance or demeanor.

What distinguishes toxic detours from other career disruptions is the lasting impact on how women trust institutions and authority figures. Long after the toxic workplace is left behind, the hypervigilance remains. The questioning of their own perceptions persists. The expectation of betrayal colors future professional relationships. These aren't just career detours—they're ruptures in how women experience their professional identities and workplace relationships.

Yet somehow, women continue. They rebuild, reconnect, and reclaim their professional power. Not because their experiences taught them resilience, but because they refused to let unfair career detours define their ultimate destination. They find ways to set down some of these burdens, or at least redistribute their weight. They learn which environments might be safe enough to reveal their authentic experiences. They develop finely-tuned sensors for detecting toxicity before it can wound them again.

Perhaps the most powerful act of resistance against the toxic detour is simply naming it for what it is. It is not a personal failure, not an inevitable part of professional life, but an injustice that constrains women's full participation in workplaces. It diminishes the integrity of organisations that allow it to flourish. By sharing these stories, we create the possibility of workplaces that, in some far off future, recognise the invisible rocks women carry and actively work to lighten that load rather than adding to it.

Karma might not deliver justice or equity, but women's collective voices, rising in recognition of these shared experiences, just might.

Gendered Roadblocks

The Starting Line Disadvantage

While previous chapters have explored specific events that disrupt women's careers—motherhood, illness, toxic workplaces—this chapter examines perhaps the most persistent detour of all: womanhood itself. Imagine setting out on a journey where every map was designed for someone else, where the terrain constantly shifts beneath your feet, and where invisible barriers appear without warning. A journey where you are not starting from the same place as men. This is the reality of navigating a career as a woman.

Unlike temporary detours that eventually allow a return to the main road, gender creates a perpetual rerouting—a continuous navigation of alternative paths simply because the direct route isn't accessible. It forces us to find ways around or over the roadblocks. It's not that women can't reach the same destinations as men; it's that they must travel farther, navigate more obstacles, and carry those damned invisible rocks while doing so.

Work for women is not the same as work for men. It is a complex blend of ever-changing societal norms swirling in a stagnant pool of historical sludge. From recruitment through to promotion, women experience gender bias. Whether it is allowable or not, certain assumptions and questions go through the interviewers' minds: "Will this 20-something year old woman need to take extended periods of maternity leave?", "Will this mother take additional days of leave to care for sick children?", "Will this woman who has been working in a lower level, lower skilled job due to family commitments be able to rise to the challenges of new technologies?", "Will this late career woman be menopausal and mean?".

Most people know better than to say these things out loud, because it is discrimination. It doesn't mean people don't silently wield their bias while maintaining the illusion of progressiveness and equality. This perpetual detour manifests in numerous ways—recruitment discrimination, pay gaps, workplace dynamics, and even conflicts between women themselves. It creates a professional landscape where women's careers aren't just occasionally disrupted by specific events, but are fundamentally shaped by gender at every step. These aren't dramatic redirections but constant, subtle adjustments—the small, daily negotiations and compromises that accumulate over decades.

What makes this detour particularly challenging is its invisibility to those who don't experience it. The barriers aren't clearly marked; they're disguised as "just the way things are," as neutral meritocracy, as reasonable expectations. The perpetual detour of gender becomes normalised to the point where many women don't recognise how their paths have been altered until they look back and map the additional distance travelled, and the additional weight carried.

The Reproductive Potential Penalty

The perpetual detour of gender becomes particularly visible when motherhood enters the equation. Actually, not even motherhood, just possessing the biological potential to become one. While having children creates career disruptions as we've explored, it's the societal response to motherhood that transforms a temporary pause into a permanent disadvantage. The mere possibility of future motherhood creates barriers even before they materialise.

June (name changed for privacy) encountered this gender-specific roadblock when attempting to re-enter the workforce after having her first child. Like many women, she had anticipated a straightforward return—settle her toddler into daycare, then resume her career. The reality proved far more complicated.

Seeking to balance her professional identity with family responsibilities, June applied for a part-time marketing role at a real estate agency. The position seemed tailor-made for her situation—flexible hours, reduced pressure, yet still within her industry. On paper, she was overqualified. In practice, she was about to discover how motherhood had fundamentally altered how employers perceived her value.

During the interview, a senior manager—ironically a middle-aged white male—began probing about her childcare arrangements for her toddler son. This initial questioning evolved into inquiries about her plans and goals for the next few years. June, focusing on professional aspirations, spoke of career development and skills growth. She was confused by the interviewer's persistent redirection toward personal matters, not immediately recognising the subtext of his questions.

The interviewer wasn't interested in her career plans. He wanted to assess the risk of future pregnancy to determine whether he might soon need to find a maternity leave replacement. Though illegal in Australia and many other places, this discriminatory calculus happens daily behind closed doors, where plausible deniability protects those who make hiring decisions based on gender and parental status.

June found herself in an impossible bind. She reluctantly provided the personal information requested, attempting to avoid appearing difficult, yet she recognised the inappropriateness of the questions. Throughout the exchange, she felt a simmering annoyance—these matters were irrelevant to her qualifications and also none of their business. The approach left her deeply uncomfortable. She was uncertain how to respond without jeopardising her chances of employment, and shocked it was something she even had to think about.

This was her first interview since having her child, and June didn't have the confidence to challenge inappropriate questioning or assert her rights, especially to a patriarchal figure in a suit. I probed as to why she hadn't reported the discrimination or at least made a complaint. She knew the interviewer would deny this as the question was not asked directly, but also she revealed another dimension of women's vulnerability: June was renting her home through this same real estate agency. She feared a formal complaint might create problems with her housing situation. The power imbalance extended beyond the interview room into her very living situation.

"Besides," she added, "that line of questioning and unethical approach told me everything I needed to know about their company culture. I realised I didn't want to work there anyway."

June's experience of facing discriminatory questions about future pregnancies during her job interview illustrates how even the potential of motherhood transforms a woman's career landscape. This roadblock isn't just about time away for childbearing—it's about navigating a professional world that views her reproductive capacity as a liability rather than a normal part of human experience. This roadblock is seen clearly when we recognise that even women who never have children, or never want them, face these biased assumptions simply because they possess the biological potential for motherhood.

Economic Tollways

Women struggle with contradictory expectations: being simultaneously penalised for motherhood yet expected to perform it perfectly, or even penalised for not having children as though it was a compulsory part of being a woman. You are damned if you do and damned if you don't. Women face a tangible economic penalty caused by the bias held about their womanhood, whether they become mothers or not.

The gender pay gap refers to the difference in average earnings between men and women in the workforce. It is not simply about women being paid less than men for the exact same job—that is illegal in many countries—but rather a reflection of systemic factors that disadvantage women economically. These include occupational segregation, where women are overrepresented in lower-paid industries like customer service, social services and healthcare, and underrepresentation in high-paying leadership roles.

Additionally, women are more likely to take career breaks or work part-time due to caregiving responsibilities, leading to lower lifetime earnings and fewer opportunities for promotions. Discrimination, unconscious bias, and a lack of workplace flexibility also contribute to the pay gap, reinforcing financial disparities that persist into retirement. The gender pay gap doesn't just affect women's earnings during their working lives—it has long-term consequences that extend into retirement. Lower wages mean lower superannuation contributions, leaving many women with significantly less savings by the time they reach retirement age. This issue is compounded for women who take time out of the workforce for caregiving responsibilities, further reducing their superannuation balance. For those without a partner to supplement household income or share living costs, the financial strain is even greater, increasing the risk of poverty in later life. As a result, many single, retired women face financial insecurity, relying on the age pension or continuing to work well beyond retirement age to make ends meet.

This economically based detour represents perhaps the most lasting consequence of gender inequality in the workplace. While June worried about securing her next position, the larger pattern shows that her decision to re-enter the workforce part-time means she will still likely face a lifetime of reduced earnings and retirement security—not because of her capabilities or contributions, but simply because she is a woman navigating a system designed with men's career patterns in mind, controlled by men.

When women earn less, take career breaks, or work in undervalued roles, they can become economically dependent in ways that may compromise their safety and autonomy. This economic dependency can manifest through daily compromises and vulnerabilities: being unable to access joint bank accounts without a partner's permission, lacking sufficient credit history to secure housing independently, remaining in unfulfilling or toxic relationships to maintain health insurance coverage, postponing necessary medical care due to inability to afford unpaid time off, or finding themselves unable to leave dangerous situations because doing so would result in immediate homelessness for themselves and their children.

The practical reality of economic dependency means calculating whether this month's paycheck could cover first and last month's rent plus security deposit—if leaving were even safely possible. It means tracking exactly how many sick days remain and whether using one for a child's illness might result in termination. It means silently tracking which bills could go unpaid if she were suddenly solo-parenting. This dependency isn't just about having less money—it's about having fewer options to make authentic choices about one's own life and safety.

Domestic violence against women represents a widespread crisis with devastating consequences for both victims and any children involved. The intersection between abuse and career disruption creates particularly complex challenges, as economic control is often a central tactic used by abusers to maintain power. Many survivors face impossible choices between financial security and personal safety. Abusers frequently sabotage their partners' employment through deliberate interference—preventing them from getting to work, creating emergencies during important meetings, or destroying work materials. The resulting missed days and unexplained absences can jeopardize women's professional standing, further isolating them from potential sources of independence and support.

The career impact of domestic violence operates through multiple interconnected mechanisms. It is not as simple as 'just leave'. Those living in domestic violence situations, and survivors, often struggle with trauma-related mental health impacts that affect work performance. Safety concerns may require frequent relocations, disrupting professional networks and employment continuity. The psychological manipulation inherent in abusive relationships can erode confidence and decision-making abilities that are crucial for career advancement.

For children who experience domestic violence, the effects can be lifelong, impacting their emotional well-being, education, and future relationships. The cycle of trauma and economic hardship often continues across generations, reinforcing inequality and limiting opportunities. Children may internalise various harmful patterns about relationships, power, and their own worth and potential.

The same economic systems that undervalue women's work and normalise career interruptions for caregiving also contribute to the conditions that can trap women in dangerous situations—demonstrating how financial independence, while not a complete solution, remains a crucial component of personal safety and autonomy.

Gatekeepers and Glass Ceilings

Systemic barriers and male-dominated power structures create significant career detours for women, but often unacknowledged in discussions of gender equality are the additional barriers women face from unexpected sources—both from other women and from being systematically underestimated by men. These internal and interpersonal detours can be particularly disorienting because they contradict our expectations of workplace fairness and feminist solidarity.

Before anyone starts throwing around accusations of man-bashing or man-hating, I want to acknowledge that abuse and disruption also happen to men. Some of the most toxic work situations I have personally experienced, echoed by many women I've interviewed, involve women undermining other women. While the magic of women supporting women is immeasurably powerful, the flip side is that women's scorn, jealousy and insecurity can create volatile situations that cause long-lasting damage. This dynamic creates a particularly treacherous detour for young, aspiring women, where seasoned female professionals who are ideally placed to mentor the next generation instead feel threatened by younger, ambitious women. Not a man in sight. Just women hating on other women and dragging each other down.

Many of the women I spoke with also felt that older men in their workplaces held unfair views about women based on their age and appearance, underestimating their capabilities while overvaluing youth and conventional attractiveness. This creates a double bind where women face skepticism from male colleagues who question their competence while simultaneously navigating potential hostility from female colleagues who view them as competition. However, these patterns aren't the same everywhere. Different industries, companies, and regions handle these issues very differently. Many workplaces are actively working to change these dynamics through new policies, training programs, and deliberate efforts to value experience and expertise over appearance and demographics.

I remember getting advice when I was younger: "Watch out for the menopausal middle managers." I was mildly insulted by this remark. Now I understand this warning differently. It should have been a warning about women who had fought hard to overcome significant career obstacles, and resented that younger women were being recognised earlier and given opportunities more readily than they had. How could they possibly be ready for leadership without "doing their time"?

This tension reflects a deeper problem rooted in artificial scarcity. When organisations signal that they'll promote 'a woman' (singular) to leadership or feature 'a female perspective' on a panel, they create conditions where women perceive each other as competitors rather than collaborators. Meanwhile, male colleagues often operate from assumptions that women—regardless of age—are less capable, creating additional barriers through lowered expectations and reduced opportunities.

This represents perhaps the most tragic aspect of women's career experiences—the cycle where those who successfully navigated earlier barriers sometimes become gatekeepers themselves, while male-dominated systems continue to underestimate women's potential. Women don't naturally aspire to undermine each other; they're responding rationally to environments where they've witnessed only one woman at a time being allowed entry to power circles. The 'queen bee' isn't born; she's created by systems that reward women for distancing themselves from other women to gain acceptance from the dominant group.

The tragedy lies in how these patterns divide potential allies, turning women who could be powerful mentors into additional barriers on an already challenging path, while male colleagues remain largely unaware of the capabilities they're overlooking.

When Excellence Isn't Enough

Jo-Ann (name changed for privacy), a young, highly driven executive, experienced workplace toxicity that illustrates how being a woman can create systematic career detours that men simply don't encounter. At the time of her most significant detour, she had been leading the marketing department for a successful retail company, spending four years there with only fantasies of leaving despite constant conflict with a condescending boss. That was until the day something inside her simply snapped.

Her physical appearance—youthful-looking and petite—became a career obstacle in ways that reveal how womanhood itself functions as a professional roadblock. As a petite woman who appeared years younger than her actual age, Jo-Ann found herself trapped in what might be called the 'cute trap'—constantly mistaken for junior staff, talked over in meetings, and subjected to diminutive descriptors that undermined her authority regardless of her competence. After back-to-back encounters with her CEO that were completely disrespectful, degrading and hostile, she responded with two words that surprised even herself: "I quit." She simply walked out the door, shocking herself with words she hadn't been contemplating but that marked one of the most impactful moments of her career.

Jo-Ann's experience demonstrates how certain combinations of female characteristics—youth, small stature, ambition—create a perfect storm of workplace challenges. She worked twice as hard to establish credibility, deliberately adjusting her communication style and appearance to command respect, only to face the classic double bind: when she displayed assertive behaviors praised in male colleagues, she was labelled as aggressive, but not assert herself: seen as weak. Clients routinely directed questions to male team members even when she was clearly in charge.

This challenge wasn't about one bad boss or toxic workplace—it was about navigating a professional world where her very identity as a young woman created a constant proving ground that detoured her career the long way around direct paths available to her male counterparts.

Jo-Ann experienced something unexpected that day she walked out of the building after quitting: an immense sense of liberation. She felt lighter and free—exactly as the cliché describes, as if a massive weight had lifted from her shoulders. Physical symptoms of stress that had become normalised—daily headaches, stomach issues, insomnia—suddenly vanished. Despite uncertainty about her future, she initially felt happier than she had in years.

Self-doubt and guilt soon crept in, but beneath these temporary reactions lay a deeper knowing: she had made one of the best decisions of her life by leaving a job that made her feel consistently miserable and diminished. The space created by this departure allowed her to reconnect with family and friends, engaging in social activities she had neglected for years. The stress of job-hunting, while substantial, paled in comparison to the daily psychological assault of a hostile workplace and toxic boss.

The aftermath of her decision that day to quit plunged Jo-Ann into a whirlwind of conflicting emotions. She felt guilty, ashamed and uncertain—emotions that speak to the particular way women internalise professional conflict. After years of fighting to be taken seriously as a woman in leadership, she found herself suddenly unemployed, emotionally fragile, and deeply questioning her professional worth in ways that reflected the cumulative toll of constantly having to prove herself.

The toxic environment hadn't just disrupted her career trajectory—it had systematically dismantled the confidence she'd worked so hard to build despite the roadblocks she had faced. For women like Jo-Ann, who already face skepticism about their authority, workplace toxicity doesn't just create professional setbacks; it attacks the self-belief they need to navigate a world that questions their competence from the start.

To rebuild her shattered confidence, Jo-Ann threw herself into education, earning a Master's Degree that would allow her to pursue work aligned with her deeper values. This sounds noble in theory, but the reality carried significant practical challenges compounded by gendered expectations. As the primary breadwinner in her household—a role that already challenged traditional expectations about women—she felt immense pressure to complete her studies and return to work quickly. Her confidence continued to waver as she questioned whether she was simply 'a person who couldn't handle tough situations,' internalising blame in a way that ignored how her gender and appearance had made those situations exponentially more difficult.

The job market proved particularly unforgiving for a young, aspiring woman carrying the invisible wounds of workplace toxicity. Jo-Ann faced more than fifty rejections while attempting to re-enter the workforce. Beyond the challenging market, she was also subconsciously sabotaging herself—holding back from applying for positions she truly wanted because years of being dismissed had convinced her that nobody would take her seriously. The roadblock she had created for herself, that of self-doubt, was seeded by external discrimination.

Jo-Ann's rebuilding process extended beyond formal education. She reworked her resume and cover letter, an exercise that forced her to acknowledge her substantial career accomplishments. She began journaling daily, capturing her experiences, future goals, and points of gratitude. These practices helped restore her sense of purpose and recentre her thoughts. Knowing she wanted to transition to work with environmental impact, she immersed herself in learning about environmental policies and topics she never had time to explore while employed. This self-directed learning rebuilt her confidence in her ability to acquire new skills and knowledge in previously unfamiliar areas.

This process of recalibration and redirection ultimately led Jo-Ann to an environmentally focused organisation where she now holds a senior leadership position and creates meaningful impact. What initially appeared to be a career-ending disruption became the very detour that redirected her toward more fulfilling work aligned with her values.

Jo-Ann's experience reveals an important truth about women's career detours: sometimes the most painful disruptions create essential space for recalibration and redirection. While we shouldn't romanticise the very real damage that toxic workplaces inflict, her story demonstrates that career detours aren't always dead-ends—sometimes they're the necessary exits that lead to more authentic professional paths.

Sacrifice

For women who have fought to establish themselves in male-dominated fields, the sacrifices demanded by motherhood carry a particularly sharp edge. These women haven't just built careers—they've broken barriers, proven themselves repeatedly in environments where their presence was questioned, and earned recognition in spaces designed to exclude them. When family obligations force them to step back, they often find themselves not just pausing their careers, but abandoning the very fields where they fought so hard to belong. The path back to their original level of expertise and recognition may be permanently blocked, leaving them to reconstruct their professional identities in roles that society deems more suitable for women—regardless of their actual talents and ambitions.

Lyn's (name changed for privacy) story begins with what appeared to be a motherhood success story in a male-dominated field. Working in a senior scientific role for an international organisation, her career initially weathered the transition to motherhood remarkably well. In a field where women rarely reached her level of expertise and recognition, she had carved out significant status and respect. Her first child seemed to integrate seamlessly into her professional life—her husband stepped into the primary caregiver role due to Lyn's frequent international travel, and she maintained her position through remote work arrangements.

This carefully constructed balance suggested that with the right support, women could maintain high-powered careers in male-dominated fields while raising children. But as many women discover, what works with one child doesn't necessarily scale to two, especially when geographic changes enter the equation.

When Lyn had her second child, her family relocated for her husband's work. In theory, she could continue her remote scientific role. Reality proved harsher. The combination of time zone differences, two small children, no external support system, and chronic sleep deprivation quickly became overwhelming. Adding to these practical challenges was debilitating social isolation—her demanding schedule left no opportunity to build local connections, trapping her in the piercing loneliness that comes when motherhood occurs without community.

Walking away from her beloved scientific career devastated Lyn professionally and personally. She had fought to establish herself in a field where women were rare, earning recognition as an acknowledged expert in her specialised area. Her professional identity was deeply intertwined with this hard-won position in what remained very much a man's world. Nevertheless, her wellbeing required a difficult compromise.

Lyn secured a much lower-level administrative job locally—work that allowed her to build a social network and align with her children's daycare hours. The shift was jarring: from using her expertise at a high level to managing filing systems, from international recognition to local anonymity. She traded late-night meetings with global colleagues and stimulating intellectual challenges for predictable hours and social interaction. While the new role addressed her isolation, the professional sacrifice was enormous. After years as a respected scientist, she found herself feeling like she had taken feminism back to the 1950's.

The ego and income adjustment proved particularly difficult. Colleagues treated her exactly as the position suggested—an entry-level administrative employee—with no knowledge of her previous achievements or capabilities.

This professional demotion came with an unexpected challenge: a micromanaging supervisor who felt threatened by Lyn's obvious overqualification. The irony wasn't lost on Lyn—having successfully navigated male-dominated scientific hierarchies, she now struggled with a female manager who saw her expertise as a threat rather than an asset. The supervisor's insecurity made it clear that Lyn's input into any decision making was unwelcome, forcing Lyn to essentially hide her skills to avoid workplace conflict.

Attempting to address the situation directly resulted in significant tension. Lyn made another difficult choice, leaving the security of this full-time position for short-term contract work that offered slightly more intellectual engagement, though still far below her capabilities. Her rationale captured the classic calculation many mothers make: being available for her children while supporting her husband's flourishing career, all while telling herself that her own career recalibration could wait.

Though Lyn had no plans for more children, the company tried to retain her with maternity leave provisions, recognising they were getting a highly qualified employee at an administrative salary. This exemplified how women's biological capabilities and reproductive potential continually factor into workplace decisions in ways men never experience.

Several years passed before Lyn secured a position that offered some professional satisfaction while maintaining family balance. Just as she achieved this precarious equilibrium, her husband received an opportunity requiring another international relocation to a country where neither she nor her children spoke the language. Ironically, never having regained her scientific stature made this decision easier. Without a position that truly captured her capabilities, pursuing this move felt less like sacrificing a thriving career and more like embracing another fresh start.

Lyn's journey illustrates the particularly brutal sacrifice women in male-dominated fields face when family obligations arise. Having fought to establish credibility in spaces designed to exclude them, these women often find that stepping back doesn't just pause their careers—it permanently severs their connection to the fields where they once excelled. The path back to their original level of expertise and recognition becomes blocked, forcing them into roles that society considers more suitable for women, regardless of their actual capabilities.

Her story reveals how motherhood can completely dismantle the professional identities women worked so hard to build in male-dominated spaces. The woman who broke barriers becomes the woman who files papers—not by choice, but by circumstance that society frames as her natural maternal instinct to put others before herself. Is this a betrayal to the greater feminist movement, or a choice that can be made because of it?

Liberation

Throughout this chapter, we've explored how being a woman creates a perpetual detour—from recruitment discrimination to pay gaps, from impossible expectations to workplace conflicts. These gender-based detours aren't occasional disruptions but continuous redirections that shape entire career trajectories. Yet the most important truth about detours is this: they may lengthen the journey, but they don't determine the destination.

When June walked away from that discriminatory interview, choosing workplace respect over any specific position, when Jo-Ann finally quit her toxic job and redefined success to include personal fulfillment alongside professional achievement, when Lyn stopped trying to recreate her former scientific career and started building something new that honored her current life priorities—these weren't just career decisions. They were acts of resistance against systems designed to diminish their worth, and acts of self-definition that prioritised authentic success over conventional metrics.

What emerged consistently across the women I interviewed was a powerful insight: there is never a 'perfect time' to redirect your path when it's no longer serving you. But waiting for the perfect moment often becomes an excuse, rooted in something deeper than practical concerns. Nobody likes a big-noter, but so many women possess particularly damaging form of self-doubt that goes beyond normal uncertainty, or even healthy humility. Unlike healthy self-doubt that prompts realistic self-assessment, it becomes a systematic erosion of your own perceptions. It's the voice that says "Everyone deals with sexist comments; I'm too sensitive" rather than recognising discrimination for what it is. It's convincing yourself that physical symptoms of workplace stress are personal weaknesses rather than warning signs of a toxic environment. It is self-betrayal.

The depth of effort required to be a successful woman transforms success into something beyond mere accomplishment—it becomes validation, vindication, and reclamation of professional space. When June walked away from that discriminatory interview, when Jo-Ann finally quit her toxic job, when Lyn stopped trying to recreate her former career and started building something new—these weren't just career decisions. They were acts of resistance against systems designed to diminish their worth.

Perhaps the most damaging barrier on these detours is the erosion of confidence that inevitably accompanies them, undermining even the strongest women's potential and stopping progress before it begins. The psychological toll creates invisible but overwhelming internal barriers that can be as formidable as any external discrimination. Rebuilding this depleted confidence becomes crucial work, requiring not just individual resilience but supportive networks that consistently reinforce a woman's fundamental right to aspire and achieve. True empowerment stems from believing in one's own capabilities as deeply as having them recognised by others—and sometimes, as these women discovered, believing in yourself first becomes the foundation for demanding that recognition from the world. The roadblocks created by gender may be perpetual, but need not define the entire journey. When women recognise these roadblocks as systemic barriers rather than personal failings, they stop blaming themselves for the additional distance they must travel and start building new routes around the obstacles that honor both their professional ambitions and their full humanity.

The Unmapped Path

Charting the Journey

Throughout this book, we've traveled alongside women navigating various career detours—from the biological redirections of motherhood to the confrontations with mortality that come through illness and grief, from the unfair distribution of hardship in the karmic detour to the perpetual adjustments required by gender itself. Each story has revealed not just the obstacles women face, but the remarkable resilience they demonstrate in finding their way back to meaningful work and purpose.

The women whose journeys we've followed have encountered different barriers, carried different configurations of invisible rocks, and discovered different paths forward. Yet across their diverse experiences, certain truths emerge with striking clarity. Career disruptions are rarely just professional pauses—they're recalibrations that affect identity, confidence, and purpose. The way forward is never straightforward, never follows a predetermined timeline, and never exactly resembles the original path.

Biological realities intersect with workplace expectations, creating complex negotiations between maternal and professional identities. Women like Kate and Nikki demonstrated that there's no single "right way" to navigate this path—some find meaning in extended career pauses while others maintain professional momentum through creative adaptations. Their stories revealed how society simultaneously expects women to be devoted mothers and dedicated professionals, without creating the structures that would make this genuinely possible.

Sudden confrontations with mortality, like losing a loved one, or facing serious illness, transform not just career trajectories but fundamental values and priorities. Hannah's and Jillian's cancer journeys and Amber's experience with loss illuminated how these disruptions forever alter one's relationship with work, sometimes diminishing capacity but often deepening empathy and perspective. These women showed us that when death enters the equation—either as immediate reality or confronted possibility—professional identity undergoes a permanent recalibration.

We also saw how unfair distribution of hardship creates seemingly random yet devastating career disruptions. Rachel's cascade of family medical crises and the toxic workplace experiences shared by others demonstrated how sometimes challenges pile up with cruel intensity, defying any sense of fairness or justice. These stories confirmed that karma doesn't reliably reward good intentions or punish harmful behaviors—sometimes good people face overwhelming obstacles while those who create harm advance unimpeded.

The most pervasive of all is gender itself. Being a woman creates a perpetual rerouting that requires extra navigation, additional energy, and continuous adaptation. June's experience with discriminatory interviewing practices and Jo-Ann's battle with authority perceptions are common examples of how gender itself becomes a daily obstacle course that must be navigated alongside professional responsibilities.

The Strength Within

The women in these stories often credit their support networks—the right people appearing at crucial moments. But external support only works when you become part of your own network. Others can provide strength, but you must translate it into forward movement, converting their faith in you into genuine self-belief. Support systems are essential, but meaningless until you join in on your own journey.

Support isn't guaranteed to appear when you need it most. Grief stories are particularly filled with rigid expectations and pressure to 'bounce back' on someone else's timeline. Consider Amber, whose husband's traumatic death left her unable to complete the mandatory CPR training that teachers must renew annually. The thought of performing life-saving techniques triggered overwhelming memories, making it impossible for her to legally supervise student excursions. Initially, her school community rallied—colleagues covered her duties, administrators understood without question that certain requirements would reactivate her trauma. Yet as months turned to years, Amber sensed a shift. No one directly suggested she should "get over it," but the unspoken message grew clearer: accommodations have limits, even for profound loss. People say to take as long as you need, that everyone processes grief differently, yet simultaneously applies subtle pressure to resume normal functioning. Ultimately, despite the initial support and understanding, Amber faced the difficult truth that moving forward required that she had to find the strength within herself to take her own painful first steps.

Believing in yourself after a career disruption isn't about ignoring the support you've received and trying to do it alone either—it's about recognising your own role in your recovery. Like Jo-Ann when she had to reinvent herself through additional study and pursue her passion despite her dwindling confidence, and like Hannah who had to accept a new normal after cancer forced a change in pace.

Beyond Self-Doubt and Guilt

Self-doubt often lingers after a setback, whispering that you aren't ready, that you'll fail, or that you're defined by what happened. This questioning of capability—"Can I still do this? Am I still valuable professionally?"—challenges your forward movement by undermining your belief in what you can accomplish. But just as support from others needs to be accepted, self-belief needs to be nurtured. It starts with small steps—testing your own strength, proving to yourself that you are more than your past, and choosing to define yourself by your resilience rather than your hardship.

Even as women overcome self-doubt about their capabilities, a different emotional burden often emerges: guilt. Guilt has a way of creeping in, no matter the choices you make. Unlike self-doubt, which questions what you can do, guilt questions what you should do or should have done. You might feel guilty for taking too long to get back on track, or for moving forward too quickly. You might feel guilty for accepting help, or for not needing as much support as others expected. But guilt serves no purpose in your healing or your progress, and it just weighs down your invisible bag of rocks even more. Letting go of guilt means accepting that your experience is yours alone—imperfect, personal, and shaped by circumstances only you fully understand. You don't owe anyone an explanation for how you've coped, and you certainly don't need to justify the time it takes to rebuild.

The stories shared are a testament to the strength of women. There are those who refuse to be defined by their setbacks, and those who refuse not to be defined by them and wear them like a hero's cape. Through their tales of resilience, determination, acceptance, and truth, these women's career detour stories provide avenues in people's thinking to discover, uplift, and support women navigating career disruption.

Whether you came here looking for inspiration, advice, or simply a connection with someone who understands, there is wisdom in these stories for everyone. They are not just narratives; they're beacons of hope, resilience, and empowerment.

There is no single path to moving forward after a career disruption, and no universal timeline for healing or rebuilding. What works for one person may not work for another, and that's okay. Some women find strength in diving back into work immediately, while others need time and space before they feel ready. Neither choice is more valid than the other. It's easy to compare your journey to someone else's and feel like you're falling behind, but the truth is, every story is unique. The key is to recognise what works for you—whether that's seeking support, setting small goals, or redefining success on your own terms—and to honor your own pace without guilt or pressure.

The most transformative act is refusing to let guilt dictate your timeline. Drop the unnecessary rocks, share the load with others, or build the strength to carry what remains—but never let guilt devour your progress. You owe no one an apology for how you heal.

Repositioning the Rocks

Getting help or putting some rocks down doesn't mean the rocks vanish—some will remain lifelong companions. But you can transform your relationship with them. The rocks of experience that once felt like crushing burdens can, with time and intention, become foundation stones for a new path forward. Women like Hannah found that her cancer experience eventually became the basis for greater empathy in leadership. Kate discovered that her extended career pause for her autistic children developed patience and perspective that accelerated her executive advancement. Even the heaviest rocks of grief, discrimination, and injustice can be repositioned from burdens carried alone to shared touchstones that connect women's experiences across generations. The question isn't whether you can eliminate all your rocks—it's whether you can transform how you carry them, and which ones you choose to carry forward.

While these stories celebrate individual women's remarkable resilience and the power of mutual support, they also reveal the need for fundamental change in how our systems and institutions respond to career disruptions. The burden shouldn't rest solely on women to navigate these detours with grace and grit. Workplaces need bereavement policies that acknowledge grief doesn't follow a schedule. Organisations need flexible approaches that recognise caregiving as valuable experience rather than a liability. Our economic structures need redesigning to stop penalising career pauses with lifetime financial consequences. Even as we honor women's extraordinary capacity to navigate these challenges, we must simultaneously work toward a world where the detours are less steep, the burdens more equitably distributed, and the invisible rocks are acknowledged by those who don't have to carry them. This isn't just about helping individual women navigate existing barriers—it's about dismantling unnecessary obstacles so future generations face fewer detours in the first place.

A Path Forward

I am honored to have been trusted with so many powerful accounts of women's strength, endurance, and solidarity. I have learned so much through this experience and feel a deep responsibility to convert this learning into ways to help other women navigating their unique but interwoven paths. I have more empathy for my own womanhood, and the obstacles I have faced, and more respect for the journeys others are on. Some are silent, some are solitary. Others are loud and inescapable. Each is distinct yet connected at the same time.

The process of documenting these women's stories has transformed me and healed me in ways I never anticipated. When I began collecting these narratives, I expected to find patterns and insights—what I didn't expect was how much they would reshape my understanding of resilience and inspire me to approach each day with gratitude and positivity. Each interview created a space where women trusted me with stories they had sometimes never fully articulated, even to themselves. In those conversations, I witnessed something remarkable: as women gave a voice to their experiences—naming the invisible rocks they'd carried and tracing the detours they'd navigated—they often discovered strength they hadn't fully recognised in themselves before. I became not just a collector of stories but a witness to women reclaiming their narratives, sometimes seeing for the first time the extraordinary courage embedded in what they had dismissed as "just getting through."

What struck me most was the universality beneath the individual contexts. Whether discussing motherhood with Beth, cancer with Hannah, compounding and unfair family crises with Rachel, or workplace discrimination with June, I heard the same core question echoed across their stories: "How do I remain authentically myself when everything I planned has been redirected?" Their answers were as diverse as their experiences, yet collectively they revealed that the journey through disruption isn't just about returning to a path—it's about discovering who you become as you navigate. These women taught me that unexpected career detours, while rarely chosen, often lead to deeper alignment between work and values when navigated with both self-compassion and determination—delivering the authentic life that felt impossible on the original path.

The womens' willingness to share not just their triumphs but their doubts, their grief, their rage, and their moments of disorientation has given me a more honest map of womanhood than any leadership manual or career guide could provide. Their stories have shown me that we all deserve workplaces that recognise our worth, that life's precious moments shouldn't be postponed, and that staying true to ourselves matters more than meeting others' expectations. For that gift of unguarded truth, I am sincerely grateful. We are not defined by our detours, but by how we navigate them.

To the women still finding their way: You've got this.

Julie

xxx

www.ingramcontent.com/pod-product-compliance
Lightning Source LLC
Chambersburg PA
CBHW020541080526
44583CB00013B/930